Macmillan/McGraw-Hill Science

ELECTRICITY AND MAGNETISM

AUTHORS

Mary Atwater
The University of Georgia

Prentice Baptiste
University of Houston

Lucy Daniel
Rutherford County Schools

Jay Hackett
University of Northern Colorado

Richard Moyer
University of Michigan, Dearborn

Carol Takemoto
Los Angeles Unified School District

Nancy Wilson
Sacramento Unified School District

Macmillan/McGraw-Hill School Publishing Company
New York   **Columbus**

MACMILLAN / McGRAW-HILL

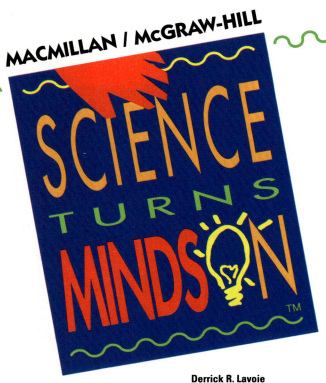

CONSULTANTS

Assessment:
Mary Hamm
Associate Professor
Department of Elementary Education
San Francisco State University
San Francisco, CA

Cognitive Development:
Pat Guild, Ed.D.
Director, Graduate Programs in Education and Learning Styles Consultant
Antioch University
Seattle, WA

Kathi Hand, M.A.Ed.
Middle School Teacher and Learning Styles Consultant
Assumption School
Seattle, WA

Derrick R. Lavoie
Assistant Professor of Science Education
Montana State University
Bozeman, MT

Earth Science:
David G. Futch
Associate Professor of Biology
San Diego State University
San Diego, CA

Dr. Shadia Rifai Habbal
Harvard-Smithsonian Center for Astrophysics
Cambridge, MA

Tom Murphree, Ph.D.
Global Systems Studies
Monterey, CA

Suzanne O'Connell
Assistant Professor
Wesleyan University
Middletown, CT

Sidney E. White
Professor of Geology
The Ohio State University
Columbus, OH

Environmental Education:
Cheryl Charles, Ph.D.
Executive Director
Project Wild
Boulder, CO

Gifted:
Dr. James A. Curry
Associate Professor, Graduate Faculty
College of Education, University of Southern Maine
Gorham, ME

Global Education:
M. Eugene Gilliom
Professor of Social Studies and Global Education
The Ohio State University
Columbus, OH

Life Science:
Wyatt W. Anderson
Professor of Genetics
University of Georgia
Athens, GA

Orin G. Gelderloos
Professor of Biology and Professor of Environmental Studies
University of Michigan—Dearborn
Dearborn, MI

Donald C. Lisowy
Education Specialist
New York, NY

Dr. E.K. Merrill
Assistant Professor
University of Wisconsin Center—Rock County
Madison, WI

Literature:
Dr. Donna E. Norton
Texas A&M University
College Station, TX

Copyright © 1995 Macmillan/McGraw-Hill School Publishing Company

All rights reserved. No part of this book may be reproduced or transmitted in any form or by any means, electronic or mechanical, including photocopying, recording, or by any information storage and retrieval system, without permission in writing from the publisher.

Macmillan/McGraw-Hill School Division
10 Union Square East
New York, New York 10003
Printed in the United States of America

ISBN 0-02-276128-4 / 6

7 8 9 RRW 99 98 97

Mathematics:
Dr. Richard Lodholz
Parkway School District
St. Louis, MO

Middle School Specialist:
Daniel Rodriguez
Principal
Pomona, CA

Misconceptions:
Dr. Charles W. Anderson
Michigan State University
East Lansing, MI

Dr. Edward L. Smith
Michigan State University
East Lansing, MI

Multicultural:
Bernard L. Charles
Senior Vice President
Quality Education for Minorities Network
Washington, DC

Paul B. Janeczko
Poet
Hebron, MA

James R. Murphy
Math Teacher
La Guardia High School
New York, NY

Clifford E. Trafzer
Professor and Chair, Ethnic Studies
University of California, Riverside
Riverside, CA

Physical Science:
Gretchen M. Gillis
Geologist
Maxus Exploration Company
Dallas, TX

Henry C. McBay
Professor of Chemistry
Morehouse College and Clark Atlanta University
Atlanta, GA

Wendell H. Potter
Associate Professor of Physics
Department of Physics
University of California, Davis
Davis, CA

Claudia K. Viehland
Educational Consultant, Chemist
Sigma Chemical Company
St. Louis, MO

Reading:
Charles Temple, Ph.D.
Associate Professor of Education
Hobart and William Smith Colleges
Geneva, NY

Safety:
Janice Sutkus
Program Manager: Education
National Safety Council
Chicago, IL

Science Technology and Society (STS):
William C. Kyle, Jr.
Director, School Mathematics and Science Center
Purdue University
West Lafayette, IN

Social Studies:
Jean Craven
District Coordinator of Curriculum Development
Albuquerque Public Schools
Albuquerque, NM

Students Acquiring English:
Mario Ruiz
Pomona, CA

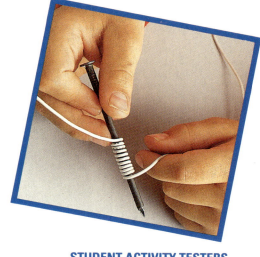

STUDENT ACTIVITY TESTERS

Alveria Henderson
Kate McGlumphy
Katherine Petzinger
John Wirtz
Sarah Wittenbrink
Andrew Duffy
Chris Higgins
Sean Pruitt
Joanna Huber
John Petzinger

FIELD TEST TEACHERS

Kathy Bowles
Landmark Middle School
Jacksonville, FL

Myra Dietz
#46 School
Rochester, NY

John Gridley
H.L. Harshman Junior High School #101
Indianapolis, IN

Annette Porter
Schenk Middle School
Madison, WI

Connie Boone
Fletcher Middle School
Jacksonville, FL

Theresa Smith
Bates Middle School
Annapolis, MD

Debbie Stamler
Sennett Middle School
Madison, WI

Margaret Tierney
Sennett Middle School
Madison, WI

Mel Pfeiffer
I.P.S. #94
Indianapolis, IN

CONTRIBUTING WRITERS

Jeff Lee
Elizabeth Alexander

ACKNOWLEDGEMENTS

WIRES AND WATTS: Understanding and Using Electricity by Irwin Math. (New York: Macmillan, 1981).

Reprinted with permission of Bradbury Press, an affiliate of Macmillan, Inc. from *THE SECRET LIFE OF DILLY McBEAN* by Dorothy Haas. Copyright © 1986 by Dorothy F. Haas.

A power substation

Electricity and Magnetism

Lessons   **Themes**

Unit Introduction   **Electricity and Magnetism** .... **Energy** **6**
You use electricity every day. What would your life be like without electricity?

1   **What Gives Matter a Charge?** .... **Energy** **10**
Static cling strikes again. What causes your pants to cling to your socks after you remove them from the clothes dryer?

2   **How Does Electrical Energy Get Around?** .... **Energy** **20**
A behind-the-walls look at how electricity gets from the switch to the ceiling light.

3   **How Do You Make Electricity Do What You Want?** ..... **Energy** **32**
What kinds of materials conduct electricity? What kinds don't?

4   **What's the Best Pathway For Electrons?** .... **Energy** **42**
Find out how to wire a string of lights so that one can burn out and the rest keep shining.

5   **How Can You Stop the Flow of Electricity?** .... **Energy** **50**
Discover several ways to control the flow of electricity.

6   **How Are Electricity and Magnetism Related?** .... **Energy** **60**
You can use electricity to make a magnet.

7   **Where Does Electric Power Come From?** .... **Energy** **72**
What do power plants and batteries have in common?

Unit Wrap Up   **Electricity at Home** .... **Energy** **86**
How has electricity in homes changed over time? What would you do in case of an electrical emergency?

Activities!

EXPLORE

Opposites Attract, Likes Repel	12
Make It Flow	22
Will It Conduct?	34
Find the Right Pathways!	44
Stopping the Flow	52
Making Electromagnets!	62
Putting Electricity To Work	74

TRY THIS

Make Puffed Cereal Do a Dance	15
Sparks Fly	18
Measuring Voltages	26
A Coat of Copper	39
It Keeps Going and Going	46
Observe Your Service Panel	56
Observing Magnetic Fields	65
A Magnetic Current	68
Tea From Sunlight	84
Your Home's Circuits	86

Features

Links

Literature Link
Science in Literature	8
Wires and Watts	41
The Secret Life of Dilly McBean	81

Social Studies Link
Fishing for Lightning	18
Setting a Compass	67
Choosing Not To Use Electricity	88

Math Link
Calculating the Current	29
This Car Runs on Batteries, Not Gasoline	48
Paying the Price for Olympic Gold	80

Health Link
Fire From a Wire	37
Preventing a Drain on Your Brain	57

GLOBAL PERSPECTIVE
It Opened the World	61

CAREERS
Electroplater	40
Electronic Service Technician	69

SCIENCE TECHNOLOGY and Society

Focus on Technology
Electricity Is Important	30
Conductors Without Resistance	38
Electronic Surveillance	70

Focus on Environment
Go With the Flow?	82

Departments

Glossary	90
Index	93
Credits	95

Electricity and Magnetism

Can you imagine how your life would be different if there were no electricity? Think about how many electrical appliances and devices you take for granted. Without a refrigerator, how would you keep food from spoiling? Without a radio, how would you hear the latest music?

Minds On! If you could have only five electrical devices, what would they be? Write a list in your *Activity Log* on page 1. Then compare your list with those that other students made. See if you can come up with a class list titled "Top 5." If you were living in Pakistan, how do you think you'd respond? ●

How small can something be? What comes to your mind when you think of a small object? Perhaps a grain of sand seems very small to you. Or maybe a grain of sand doesn't seem small because you know that each sand grain is made of a huge number of atoms. You can probably think of three objects even smaller than an atom. What do you call these objects? Scientists have given them the names *proton*, *neutron*, and *electron*. One of these three objects or particles is much smaller than the other two. Do you remember which one it is?

Besides being much smaller than protons and neutrons, electrons also move more. Everyone has noticed electrons moving from one place to another place. Have you ever touched a doorknob after shuffling your feet on a carpet? Have you ever seen a flash of lightning? Have you ever watched the burner on an electric stove change color? If you can say yes to any of these questions, then you've noticed electrons changing places.

Minds On! Perhaps you can think of other words that have the same first letters as the word *electron*. How many words can you think of? Write these in your *Activity Log* on page 2 •

Besides being smaller than the neutron and the proton, is an electron different in any other way? Scientists have discovered that electrons and protons have electric charges and neutrons don't. What words do we use to describe the charges on protons and electrons? Write these words next to the words *electron* and *proton* on a piece of paper.

Remember that when you studied forces you learned two objects with mass have a force of attraction between them known as gravity. This force of attraction can be demonstrated easily using a book and your desk. When you drop a book, it falls because of the attraction of Earth's gravitational field.

Like the book and Earth, the electron and proton are only slightly attracted to one another by gravity. Unlike the book and Earth, the electron and the proton have an electric charge. Particles having an electric charge produce another force. The study of electricity and magnetism examines what this electrical force is like and how it can be used to obtain energy or do work in different systems. What do you think electricity and magnetism are like? How do they do work?

This machine, a Van de Graaff generator, produces electrical discharges. The sparks indicate that electrons are moving from one sphere to the other.

7

Literature  Link

Science in Literature

In the books on these two pages, you'll find both stories and information about specific kinds of energy—electricity and magnetism—and how they can affect your life. Maybe you think you seldom or never have much to do with electricity and magnetism. Well, you might change your mind when these books introduce you to the possibilities.

The Secret Life of Dilly McBean by Dorothy Haas.
New York: Bradbury Press, 1986.

This novel tells of a year in the life of a teenage boy who has a unique ability: he has magnetic hands. He can pick up metal objects without bending his fingers, just like a magnet, and like an electromagnet, he can turn off the magnetism to drop the items. Spies want his secret (will they discover it?); a gang of international kidnappers targets him (but Dilly's friends and loyal dog Contrary frustrate their evil plot); and through it all, Dilly keeps practicing and refining his odd skills. This is a story for anyone who has ever wanted to be a superhero.

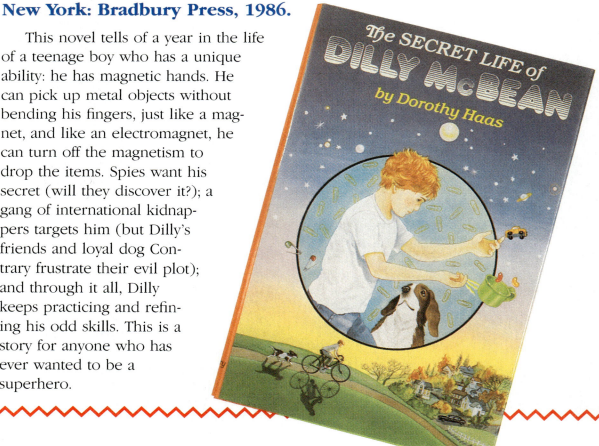

8

Wires and Watts: Understanding and Using Electricity by Irwin Math. New York: Macmillan, 1981.

The principles of electricity are clearly presented for beginners in this handbook. Using easily-available materials such as tin can metal parts, broom straws, modeling clay, and magnets, a home experimenter can build such tools and devices as switches, voltage/current indicators, lamps, alarms, motors, and even model railroad semaphores. Some readers will find that the projects lead to future careers in electricity; all will find many of the mysteries of electricity explained.

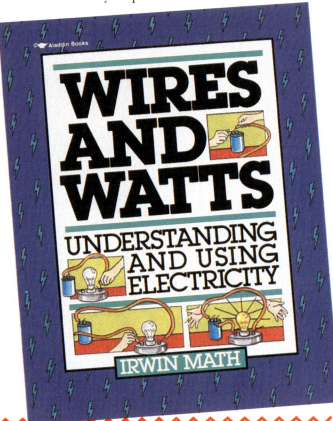

Other Good Books To Read

Superconductivity: From Discovery to Breakthrough by Charlene W. Billings. New York: Dutton, 1991.

Superconductive materials allow electricity to flow through them without any loss of energy. This book explains the discovery of superconducting materials and the long work to find uses for them—in computers, in power transmission, in medicine, in transportation, and in communication.

Blinkers and Buzzers: Building and Experimenting with Electricity and Magnetism by Bernie Zubrowski. New York: Morrow Junior Books, 1991.

Have you ever wanted to make a burglar alarm or a telegraph? How about a buzzer or a traffic light? Follow the instructions in this book to make these and other electrical devices and explore how electricity and magnetism work.

Ben and Me: An Astonishing LIFE of BENJAMIN FRANKLIN by his good mouse AMOS by Robert Lawson. Boston: Little, Brown and Company, 1939.

Did you know Benjamin Franklin got all his best ideas from a talking mouse who lived in his fur cap? This humorous novel shows us all the "real" truth behind Franklin's famous experiments, including the one that could easily have killed him. The energy in a lightning bolt is no toy, as Amos the mouse discovers when he finds himself an unwilling passenger on a kite one rainy night.

Simple Electrical Devices by Martin J. Gutnik. New York: Franklin Watts, 1986.

Clear directions and diagrams make an easy-to-use handbook for anyone who wants to learn how to build and use uncomplicated electrical tools like early telephones, light bulbs, and simple motors.

What Gives Matter a Charge?

What happens if electrons are added to or taken away from an object? In this lesson, you'll learn how to give a charge to different objects and see how that changes their energy. You'll also observe the behavior of charged objects and discover how to tell whether the charges are similar or different.

Look at the pictures on these pages. What's going on? You might think the girl in this picture is watching a movie so scary it made her hair stand on end. Or is she experimenting with a new hairdo?

What about the picture on the next page? Why are the socks that have been tumbled in the dryer clinging to each other? Surely they aren't trying to fold themselves into pairs!

Minds On! In your *Activity Log* on page 3, write an explanation for what's happening in each picture. Compare your explanations with those of your classmates. Hint: Remember that atoms make up all matter, including the matter in hair, combs, clothes, and the hot air that circulates in dryers. Think about electrons that move around the nucleus of an atom but can also move from one atom to another. Imagine what might happen to an electrically-neutral object (one with the same number of protons and electrons) if it gained some electrons. Imagine what might happen to an electrically-neutral object if it lost some electrons. Now look at the photographs again. •

In the following activity, you'll explore for yourself how electrons move around.

This girl is having a hair-raising experience.

10

What makes socks fresh from the dryer cling to each other? Is it like magnetism? Not exactly, but magnetism is a good guess.

EXPLORE

Activity!

Opposites Attract, Likes Repel

Under normal conditions, electrons don't move from object to object. They have to be made to move, which is something you can do. By making electrons move and observing what happens when they do, you can form a scientific explanation of why objects such as the ones pictured on page 11 sometimes draw toward or pull away from each other. In this exploration, you're going to investigate how matter can become electrically charged and how charged objects interact with other objects.

What You Need

2 balloons
thread
masking tape
piece of wool cloth
Activity Log pages 4–5

What To Do

1 Working in groups of two, blow up two balloons and tie them to separate pieces of thread.

2 Set balloon 1 aside. Hang balloon 2 by the thread from the edge of a desk. Use a piece of tape to hold the thread in place.

3 Bring balloon 1 near the hanging balloon. Do the balloons interact with each other? Write your observation in your **Activity Log**.

4 One member of the group should electrically charge the hanging balloon by rubbing it several times with the wool cloth. The other member should electrically charge balloon 1 in the same way.

5 Bring balloon 1 toward the hanging balloon. Write down your observations in your **Activity Log**.

6 Now, bring the wool cloth near the hanging balloon. Write down what you observe in your **Activity Log**.

7 Hang balloon 1 from the edge of the desk. Tape the string to the desk so that the balloons hang about 6 cm from one another.

8 Remove the charge from one of the balloons by rubbing both hands over the balloon. Have your partner hold the other balloon out of the way.

9 Bring the charged balloon close to the uncharged one. Record your observations in your **Activity Log**.

What Happened?

1. Were your results for steps 5 and 6 different? If they were, what was the difference?
2. Describe what happened in step 9 when you brought the charged balloon close to the uncharged one.

What Now?

1. Think about electrons. How did you make electrons move from one type of matter to another in this activity?
2. What happens to an electrically-neutral object, such as the balloon at the beginning of the activity, if it gains or loses electrons?
3. See if you can use the terms *static electricity* and *charge* to explain what you observed in this activity. (Hint: The title of the activity is a clue.) Don't worry if you have trouble. You'll learn more about this in the next few pages.

EXPLORE

13

Charged Behavior

Think about what happened in step 5 of the Explore Activity. When you brought the charged balloons near each other, what happened? The balloons **repelled,** or moved away from, each other. What happened in step 6 when you brought the charged wool close to the charged balloon? They were **attracted** and moved toward each other. What causes objects to be attracted or repelled?

Opposite charges attract. Like charges repel. Before you rubbed the balloon with wool, the balloon was electrically neutral. The atoms of the balloon had an equal number of protons and electrons. When you rubbed the balloon with wool, you caused electrons to move from the wool onto the balloon. By causing more electrons to pile up on the balloon as you rubbed it, you gave the balloon electrical charges. The balloon was negatively charged, and the wool was positively charged. When objects such as the wool cloth and the balloon gain or lose electrons so that they have more or fewer electrons than usual, we say they are charged with **static electricity**.

Objects gain static charges by **contact**, as when you rubbed the balloon with the wool. Here's another example of how objects gain static charge by contact. When the girl combs her hair, she makes electrons move from her hair onto the comb. The balance between protons and electrons in her hair and in the comb is upset. Both objects become charged. How can you tell from the picture that the hair and comb have attained opposite charges?

Do the following activity to see more effects of static electricity.

Rubbing a comb through hair is like rubbing a balloon with wool.

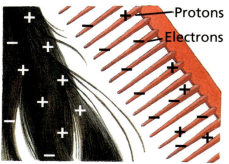

Before combing, the hair and the comb are neutral.

After combing, electrons have moved from the hair to the comb.

14

TRY THIS Activity!

Make Puffed Cereal Do a Dance

You can show the effects of static electricity on pieces of puffed cereal.

What You Need
aluminum foil
puffed grain cereal
piece of wool or silk cloth
clear plastic box
Activity Log page 6

First, tear off a sheet of aluminum foil larger than the plastic box. Take a handful of puffed cereal and lay it on the foil. Cover the cereal with the upside-down plastic box. Now, rub the bottom of the upside-down plastic box vigorously with the wool or silk cloth. What do you see happening? Depending on the humidity in the room, it may take a minute or two to get results. Why does this happen? Draw a diagram in your **Activity Log** to show what's happening.

Now think back to steps 8 and 9 in the Explore Activity, in which you removed the charge from one balloon by holding it in your hands. What about the second balloon? You didn't touch it, but when you brought the two balloons close together they attracted each other. Did the second balloon still have a charge?

A charged object, such as the second balloon, can induce, or cause, a separation of charge on an electrically-neutral object, such as the first balloon. The second object remains electrically neutral overall, but it experiences a separation of charges. For this reason, the two balloons were attracted to one another.

When you made the puffed cereal do a dance, you also caused a separation of charges in the puffed cereal. Rubbing the plastic box gave a charge to the box. The box then induced the charges to separate on the neutral puffed cereal pieces. The cereal seemed to dance because the upward surface of the cereal pieces had a charge that was opposite to the charge on the box.

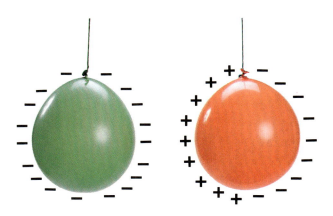

The charges on an uncharged balloon separate when a charged balloon is near.

15

Electric eel
Frog

A static discharge from the eel can kill or stun another animal.

Have you ever seen an electric eel in an aquarium? The electric eel, a fish that lives in rivers in South America, creates electricity in the muscles of its body. By passing static charge to a fish it wants to eat, the electric eel uses electricity to kill or stun its prey.

Charge can be lost by **grounding,** providing a path for electrons to flow from a charged object to another object. The transfer of static charge from one object to another is **static discharge**.

Safety experts don't worry about grounding small static discharges such as the crackle that you sometimes hear with static on clothing that has been tumbled dry. They certainly don't worry about the electric eel passing a charge to its prey! However, safety experts do concern themselves about large static discharges such as lightning, which are extremely dangerous.

Before a storm begins, electric charge builds up in a cloud when droplets of water and ice strike each other.

Separation of charge then takes place in the cloud. The bottom of the cloud becomes negatively charged compared with the ground beneath.

Cloud-to-ground lightning strikes occur when the negative charge jumps from the bottom of the cloud to the highest point on the ground. The flow of charge is so enormous that it heats the air, causing the noise we call thunder.

Neutral cloud

Cloud with separated charges

16

Discharging Without Damage

Metal lightning rods extend above the highest point of a roof and connect to metal cables near the ground. Lightning rods prevent houses and buildings from being damaged by the large amounts of electrical energy in lightning. These lightning rods provide a safe path, or **ground**, for lightning to follow into Earth rather than into a house or building. Have you ever seen a lightning rod?

Computer repair persons ground themselves by wearing a grounding strap. A grounding strap uses a wire to connect the repair person's wrist to the ground. Grounding helps to prevent any accumulation of charges that could damage delicate parts of a computer by causing them to melt or crack.

Minds On! Look back to the explanations you wrote in your **Activity Log** on page 3 for what was happening in the pictures on pages 10 and 11. How has what you just learned about static electricity changed your ideas? Write new explanations on page 7 of your **Activity Log** for those that need to be changed. ●

During a thunderstorm, the static discharge from the bottom of the thundercloud to Earth will strike this metal lightning rod. The electrical charge will travel safely down the rod, through the metal cable, and into the ground.

Metal lightning rod

Metal cable

17

Social Studies Link

Fishing for Lightning

Many people other than scientists have made important contributions to our understanding of energy. Benjamin Franklin was such a person. Primarily a journalist and a businessperson, Franklin was also an amateur scientist and a well-known political figure. You may remember him best as the person who secured French help for the American colonies in 1778, during the Revolutionary War. He was also a delegate to the Constitutional Convention in 1787.

Franklin invented the lightning rod in 1752, the same year in which he and his son performed an incredibly dangerous experiment flying a kite in a lightning storm. Perhaps you have heard this story before. Here's what happened:

Franklin wanted to find out whether lightning and electricity were the same thing. In order to do that, he took his son "fishing" for lightning. First they made a silk kite with a pointed wire at the top and a metal key tied to the end of the kite string. Then, during a lightning storm, they flew the kite high into the sky. The string became wet in the rain, providing a path for electricity to travel. Sure enough, when a storm cloud approached the kite, the kite string stiffened. A static charge from the cloud moved down the wet string to the metal key on the end of the kite. Franklin touched the key and felt a shock. He could easily have been killed! The experiment confirmed Franklin's hypothesis that lightning is indeed a form of electricity.

Do the following activity to observe a safer static discharge through a key.

TRY THIS Activity!

Sparks Fly

You can see for yourself how static charge can move from one object to another. You can collect electrons on your shoes and touch another object or person. Here's how:

What You Need

carpeted room, metal key or nail, *Activity Log* page 8, metal doorknob

Darken the room by turning out the lights and closing the window shades. While holding the key or nail in your hand, shuffle your feet across the carpet. Touch a metal doorknob with the key or nail. What did you see? What did you feel? Identify the charged object that transferred static charge to another object. Write your observations in your ***Activity Log***.

18

Lightning often eludes, or remains outside the reach of, scientists who want to study it. Although lightning strikes somewhere on Earth 100 times every second, scientists cannot depend on knowing precisely where it will strike. Moreover, as Franklin's experiment showed, lightning is hard to study under safe conditions. Some scientists who study lightning work in specially-protected buildings.

What makes lightning so dangerous? Negative charges build up on the bottom sides of dark thunderclouds. Lightning strikes when the electrons on the negatively-charged clouds rapidly jump toward the ground, which is positively charged. Lightning can also jump from cloud to cloud, or from the ground to a positively-charged cloud. A bolt of lightning is simply a much greater form of static discharge than the one you saw when you charged your shoes on the carpet and touched a doorknob. Don't ever try to repeat Franklin's experiment! It could be fatal.

Sum It Up

In this lesson, you've discovered that static charges can be placed on objects by contact. Two objects with like charges will repel each other, and two objects with unlike charges will attract each other. As you discovered when you experimented with two charged balloons, the transfer of charge by contact occurs when two objects touch each other. One of the objects will transfer electrons to the other object. The electrons move from object to object following rules, so that the way they change makes a pattern you can learn.

Separation of static charge occurs when a charged object is brought close to an uncharged object but doesn't touch it. The uncharged object remains electrically neutral overall but experiences a separation of charges. You also learned that charge can be neutralized or lost through grounding, and that lightning is a large discharge of electricity. You even felt a very small lightning bolt when you touched a metal object to a metal doorknob. Now you're ready to observe other forms of electrical energy.

Critical Thinking

1. Your teacher shows you two balloons. She tells you one is charged; it was rubbed with wool. The other balloon, she says, has no charge. How can you decide which has the charge?

2. Sara's dad put a spoonful of dry instant coffee into a dry plastic foam cup. Sara noticed that the little pieces of dry instant coffee jumped around in the cup and some stuck to the sides. Explain what happened.

3. Use the concept of static discharge to explain why it's dangerous to take shelter under a tall tree during a lightning storm.

4. Billy told his mom, "I can move these plastic cars on my desk without touching them. I bet you can't." What's his secret?

5. Imagine you're an engineer who works at a toll road where people pay money to drive on the road. Several toll collectors say they receive an electric shock every time someone hands them money. What's causing this problem? What are some possible solutions?

How Does Electrical Energy Get Around?

Electrons need a continuous path to move from one place to another. In this lesson, you'll learn how to make complete circuits that give a continuous path for electrons. You'll also learn how the push, the current, and the resistance influence the movement of electrons in a complete circuit.

Electricity influences the daily lives of people throughout the world. Many of us depend on electrical devices to make our lives safer, healthier, easier, and more enjoyable. Refrigerators, radios, vacuum cleaners, electric guitars, and video games are only a few of these devices. People who use electrical devices often depend on them. They don't even notice them most of the time—until something goes wrong.

Have you ever looked inside an electrical device when it was unplugged? If you have, you've probably seen all sorts of objects connected to each other by wires or metallic pathways. The picture at the right shows the insides of some electrical devices. The actual workings of these devices are complex. Scientists, engineers, and technicians spend years developing and improving them. But the flow of electricity through all these devices is controlled by simple rules you can learn.

Minds On!
On page 9 of your *Activity Log,* list electrical devices you use. Do you know how electricity makes them work? Try to describe how the electricity flows through one of them. ●

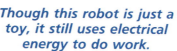

Though this robot is just a toy, it still uses electrical energy to do work.

20

The insides of these devices provide electricity with pathways that twist and turn.

21

EXPLORE Activity!

Make It Flow

In this exploration, you're going to try to use the flow of electricity to light a small bulb.

What You Need

- 2 1.5-V cells with holders
- 1 2.5-V bulb with holder
- 3 20-cm lengths of insulated copper wire
- 10-ohm resistor
- 2 alligator clips
- *Activity Log* pages 10–11

What To Do

1 Using only 1 piece of wire and 1 cell, try to make the bulb light. Record in your *Activity Log* the different ways you try. Keep track of which ways make the bulb light and which do not.

2 After you find one way to make the bulb light, see if you can find any other ways.

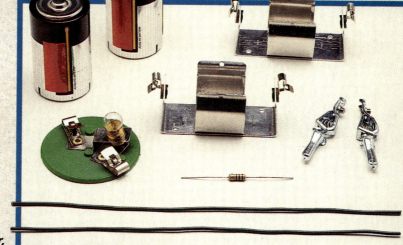

From top left to bottom: 1.5-V cells, cell holders, alligator clips, 2.5-V bulb with holder, 10-ohm resistor, insulated copper wire

3 In your *Activity Log,* draw a way that you think will work to light the bulb using 2 cells. Test your idea.

4 Make a sketch in your *Activity Log* of how you could use the holders to make 1 cell light 1 bulb. Test your idea.

5 Using the holders, find a way to light the bulb using both cells.

6 After you've made a circuit with 2 cells and 1 bulb, remove one of the wires to the bulb. Using the alligator clips, replace it with the resistor. What happened to the brightness of the bulb?

What Happened?

1. Describe one way to light a bulb using 1 wire and 1 cell.
2. Think of all the ways that worked to light the bulb in step 2. How were all the ways alike?
3. What happened to the brightness of the bulb when you added a resistor to the circuit?

What Now?

1. Tell about some ways that didn't work to light the bulb. Were they alike in any way?
2. When was the bulb lit the brightest? Why do you think this is so?
3. What happens to the bulb when you disconnect one of the wires? Why?
4. Think about the systems you've been making. Why do you think they are called electrical circuits?

EXPLORE

Pushing and Resisting a Current

In the Explore Activity, you discovered how to make a simple circuit. In order to make the bulb light, you had to provide a continuous path with the wires by connecting wires from each end of the cell to the base on the side of the bulb and to the small metal tip at the bottom of the bulb. You could follow the pathway with your finger. You saw that it was a complete path like a circle.

What do we need to produce electricity we can use? First, we need electrons. Then, we need a way to make them move. Remember how you made electrons move in Lesson 1 when you rubbed balloons with the wool cloth? You know you can't use the electricity you made in Lesson 1 to light a bulb or run a television. In order to produce electricity you can use, you have to do what you did in the activity on the previous two pages. You have to provide a continuous path, or **circuit** (sûr´ kit), for electrons.

Think about which arrangements of the cell and wires did not work. The bulb wouldn't light when the circuit had a gap in it—for example, when one of the wires wasn't connected to the negative terminal of the cell, or when one of the wires wasn't connected to the bulb. A circuit with a gap in it is a broken, or **open**, circuit. In an **open circuit** there is no path for moving electrons, and they can't make their way around to light a bulb, run an electric train, or turn the blades on a fan. The circuits you made worked when there was no gap in the path made by the cell and wires. The electrons could make their

If the bulb lights, the circuit is closed.

way all around. When all the necessary connections are made between the parts of a circuit, we call this a **closed circuit.**

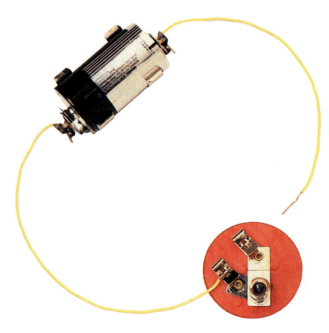

Electrons do not flow in an open circuit.

24

Minds On! Think about the circuits you made in the Explore Activity. Can you name the parts, or elements, of the circuits? (Hint: The elements of a circuit consist of all the things that it needs to work plus the device that it powers.)

Which circuits in the activity were open and which were closed? How could you tell? Write what you found out in your **Activity Log** on page 12.

Think again about the activity with the balloons in Lesson 1. You caused electrons to pile up on the balloon as you rubbed it with the wool cloth. The extra electrons on the balloon were static electricity, electricity that stays in one place.

Now think about the Explore Activity in this lesson. You made electrons move around a circuit. Which way did the electrons go around the circuit? Because like charges repel one another, the electrons moved from a place where there were more of them—the negative terminal of the battery—to a place where there were fewer of them—the positive terminal.

The flow of electrons around a circuit is known as **current electricity,** or electricity that flows. Electricity, like water, doesn't flow by itself. A city pumps water into a water tower that is above the houses in the city. The water in the water tower has more potential energy than the water in the pipes in the houses below the tower. The water will flow to the houses when a pipe provides a path for it. If the pump stops pumping water and the water tower becomes empty, water will no longer flow in the pipes. The pump works as the push behind the water current. The push in an electric circuit comes because there is a difference in the potential (pə ten′ shəl) energy of the electrons in two places. **Potential difference** occurs when electrons with more potential energy in one place (negative end of an electron source such as a battery) can go to a place where the electrons have less energy (positive end of an electron source such as a battery). We measure potential difference in units called **volts.** Potential difference is also known as **voltage.** The cell that pushed electrons around the circuit you made had a low potential difference of only 1.5 volts. Most homes have circuits with either 120 volts or 220 volts. Do the following Try This Activity to examine the potential difference of some common cells.

Pushing a current in a string of lights produces heat and light.

TRY THIS Activity!

Measuring Voltages

How do the voltages of D, C, AA, and AAA cells compare?

What You Need
volt meter (0–3V)
1 D cell, 1 C cell, 1 AA cell, and
  1 AAA cell
2 20-cm lengths of insulated
  copper wire
Activity Log page 13

Connect 1 copper wire to the positive side of the voltmeter. Connect the second copper wire to the negative side. Now, touch the unattached ends of the wires to the positive and negative sides of a D cell (positive to positive and negative to negative). Repeat this procedure with a C cell, an AA cell, and an AAA cell. Does a larger cell always give more voltage? Write your observations in your **Activity Log**.

The pump in this water system gives a "push" to the water. The water moves from the pump, around a path, and back to the pump. How is this water system similar to an electrical circuit?

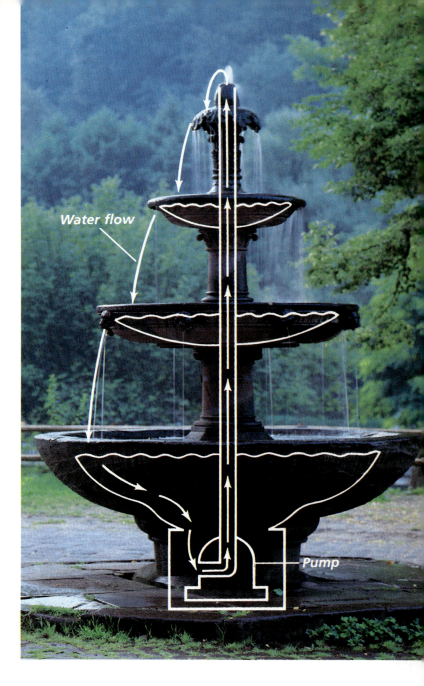

Water flow

Pump

Where did the electrons flowing around your circuit in the Explore Activity come from? Batteries are one source of electric current. You've probably been using batteries to cause a current for a long time. Generators are another source of electric current. You'll learn more about generators in Lesson 7.

Look at the diagram of a large water system. Think about how a water system and an electric circuit are alike. Just as some pumps give more push to the water than other pumps, some electric circuits have more volts or give more push to the current electricity than others. Current in an electric circuit is like water in a water system. Some systems allow more water to flow than other systems. Some circuits carry more electrons than others.

A closed system you may already know about is similar to a closed circuit and is located in our bodies. The **circulatory system** consists of the heart and blood vessels. Think about your heart. How is it like the battery in the circuit you made? You know that your heart pumps blood in a loop around your body. The heart pumps a great deal of blood— 4,750 to 5,700 liters (5,000 to 6,000 quarts) per day! The heart pushes blood through your circulatory system just as the battery pushed electrons through the electric circuit. In the electric circuit, you used wire to carry the electrons around. In your circulatory system, blood vessels are the "wires" that carry oxygen-rich blood out to all parts of your body and return oxygen-poor blood to your lungs.

Minds On! On a simple drawing of the circulatory system, label the parts that are similar to the elements of an electric circuit. Add this labeled drawing to your **Activity Log** on page 14. •

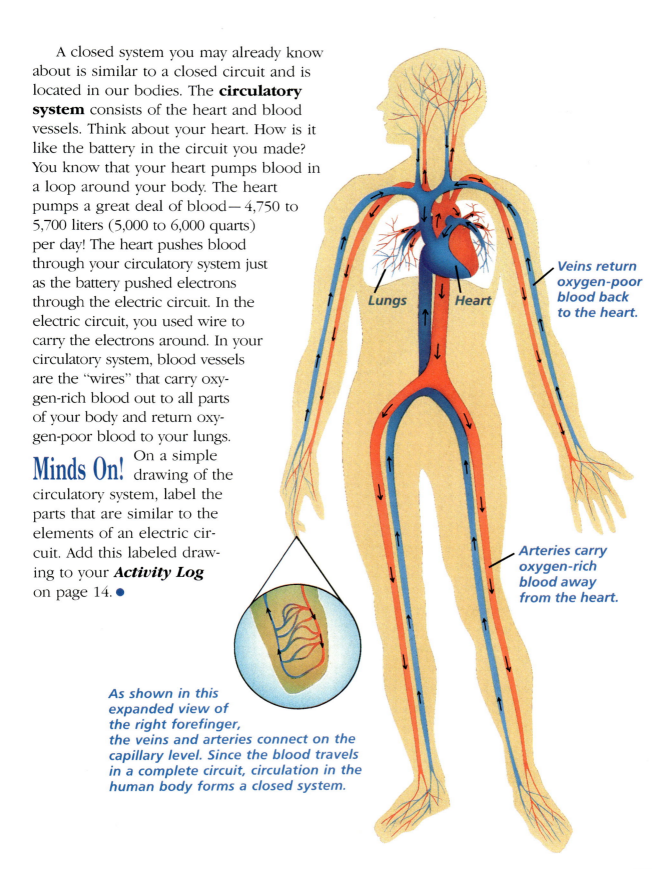

Lungs **Heart**

Veins return oxygen-poor blood back to the heart.

Arteries carry oxygen-rich blood away from the heart.

As shown in this expanded view of the right forefinger, the veins and arteries connect on the capillary level. Since the blood travels in a complete circuit, circulation in the human body forms a closed system.

27

Resistance to electric current releases energy in the form of heat.

In your circuits in the Explore Activity, you observed changes in how bright the bulb was. The brightness depended on whether one or two cells were used in the circuit. This is because two cells provided more push to the electric current. Two cells can give twice as much push, or voltage, as one cell.

Why wasn't the bulb as bright after you replaced one of the wires with a carbon resistor? Using a carbon resistor in the circuit causes the bulb to burn less brightly because there is less electric current. The carbon resistor gives more opposition or resistance to the electric current than a copper wire does. To keep the same current, more push or voltage is needed when circuit elements give more resistance. In an electric circuit, the measure of how the elements slow down or resist the current is called **resistance**. An example of a circuit element with a large resistance is the burner on an electric stove. Resistance is measured in **ohms**. The ohm is named after Georg S. Ohm, who studied how electric current, push, and resistance are related. This relationship is known as **Ohm's Law**. Ohm's Law says if you increase the push you increase the current, and if you increase the resistance you decrease the current. Ohm's Law explains why your bulb burned more brightly when you added a cell and less brightly when you used a carbon resistor.

Current (More or Less?)

Think about the importance of resistance in some common electrical devices. You know electrons must have a big push to flow through the circuit in a toaster. Look at the toaster pictured on this page. Notice how the long resistance wire winds back and forth. The electrons are pushed easily through the low-resistance wire running from the toaster cord to the resistance wire. The resistance wire resists the flow of electrons. The high voltage is enough to move electrons through the wire despite the resistance. Electrons lose energy as heat going through the resistance wire, and the resistance wire turns red hot. As the bread is toasting, you can see the wire glow. What other electrical appliances use high resistance to make wires turn red hot?

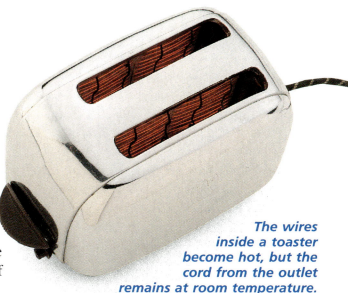

The wires inside a toaster become hot, but the cord from the outlet remains at room temperature.

Math Link
Calculating the Current

You know we use units called *volts* to measure the potential difference it takes to push electrons in a circuit. You also know we measure resistance to the flow of electrons or current in units called ohms. There is one more unit you must know in order to calculate the amount of current in a circuit. That unit is the **ampere** or amp. We use **amps** to measure the amount of current in a circuit. Many electrical appliances and devices are marked to show how many amps they use.

Using math, Ohm's Law can be stated another way. You can find the amount of current (amps) in a circuit by dividing the voltage (volts) by the resistance (ohms).

Amps = volts ÷ ohms

If you know the greatest amount of current a circuit can carry, you know how many electrical devices and appliances you can run at the same time. Engineers design every circuit to carry just the right amount of current. It's very dangerous to cause too much current to flow through a circuit. In Lesson 5, you'll find out why.

Suppose you have three circuits. Each circuit has one or two 1.5-volt cells and one miniature pump. The three circuits have different resistances depending on whether a copper wire or a carbon resistor is used.

The voltage and resistance for each circuit are given in the chart below. Complete the chart and copy it in your ***Activity Log*** on page 15. Use a calculator and Ohm's law to find the amount of current for each electric circuit.

Circuit	Potential	Resistance	Current
1	1.5 volts	5 ohms	____ amps
2	1.5 volts	15 ohms	____ amps
3	3.0 volts	15 ohms	____ amps

Minds On! Scientists often ask "What would happen if...?" to help them solve problems. You try it! Answer the following questions using Ohm's law. Write your predictions in your *Activity Log* on page 16.
1. What would happen to the electric current in a flashlight bulb if you put in a bulb with lower resistance?
2. What would happen to the current in a circuit if you increased the push?
3. What would happen to the current in a circuit if you put in a motor with a large resistance?
4. What would happen to the current in a circuit if you added another cell to increase the push?
5. What would happen to the current in a circuit if you used bigger wires that had less resistance?

Focus on Technology
Electricity Is Important
(Make No Bones About It!)

What happens if you forget to turn off the lights when getting out of a car at night? The lights drain the battery. If they remain on for very long after the car has stopped running, the battery discharges. Then what? You know that some kinds of batteries can often be recharged. Did you know that, just as some people can recharge a car battery, some doctors can recharge broken bones?

If bones can be recharged, then bones must contain electricity. And they do—sometimes. When you stress a bone by walking, running, or doing other physical activities, small electric currents are produced. The current circulating through your bones helps you stay healthy in a couple of ways. Electric pulses stimulate the bone cells causing the bones to grow. Scientists also think electricity prevents bones from being destroyed by a certain harmful material.

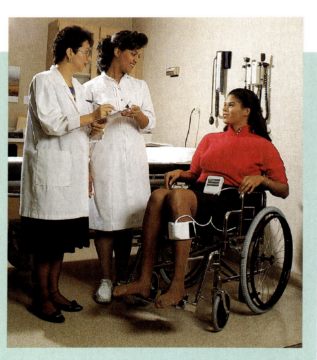

Electric pulses help heal broken bones.

Why would a broken bone need to be recharged? Well, most broken bones don't need recharging because they heal naturally. But in a few broken bones, about five percent, the natural healing process doesn't occur. Doctors can apply short bursts of electricity to aid in healing these bones. Scientists who specialize in medicine hope one day electric pulses can also be used to treat patients with diseases that destroy bones.

Sum It Up

In this lesson, you've learned that a circuit is a complete path for electrons to flow through. You discovered in the Explore Activity on pages 22 and 23 that if the continuous path is interrupted, the circuit is said to be open. Open circuits don't allow the flow of electrons through the circuit, but closed circuits do. The kind of electricity that is the flow of electrons through a circuit is called current electricity. One aspect of current electricity is the current, or the amount of electricity, that flows. Current is measured in amps. There are several sources of current electricity. One is the cell. A cell pushes the flow of electrons due to a difference in the potential energy between the ends or terminals. Potential difference or voltage, the amount of electric push, is measured in volts. You've also learned about resistance. Resistance is the opposition to the flow of electrons through matter. Resistance is measured in ohms. Current, resistance, and potential difference are related by Ohm's Law. Ohm's Law says if you increase the push, you increase the current, and if you increase the resistance, you decrease the current. Mathematically, Ohm's Law can be written as amps = volts ÷ ohms.

Now that you understand the relationship among current, resistance, and voltage, you're closer to understanding how an electrical device operates.

Critical Thinking

1. Your friend brings you a flashlight and asks you to fix it. When you push the button to turn it on, it doesn't light. List at least three things you would check.

2. A dimmer switch is often used to allow people to make a light bulb brighter or dimmer by turning a knob. The knob increases or lowers the resistance in the circuit that contains the bulb. Use what you know about Ohm's Law to explain how the amount of current might influence the brightness of a bulb.

3. An electrician checks a cord he suspects of being broken even though it looks fine. He attaches the cord to the meter, which indicates there is almost no resistance in the cord. Is the cord broken or not? Tell how you know.

4. When you close a refrigerator door, the light inside goes off. The light is turned off and on by a button near the door. Explain in terms of open and closed circuits how the light goes on and off.

5. In the water system on page 26, a pump pushed water through pipes. What parts of an electric circuit are these parts of a water circuit like—the pump? The pipes? The water?

How Do You Make Electricity Do What You Want?

Does a river always flow no matter what gets in its way? Does electricity always flow, or can some materials stop its flow? In this lesson, you'll test different materials to determine whether electrons can easily flow in them.

Think about the verb *conduct*. A tour guide *conducts* members of a tour by keeping the members together and leading them through the building. Now, think about a wire. Does a wire conduct electrons through a circuit?

When you constructed a circuit in the previous lesson, you used wire through which the electrons could flow. The flow of electrons through a wire is like the flow of cars on a road. Some wires, like some roads, are better conductors than others. It's easier for a car to travel on a paved street than a dirt road. It's easier for electrons to move through a copper wire than through the same size of aluminum wire. It's easier for the same number of cars to move on a four-lane highway than on a two-lane highway. (The cars on the four-lane highway have less resistance to their movement.) Likewise, it's easier for electrons to move in a thick wire than in a thin wire of the same material. More current flows in a thick wire.

A thicker wire is a larger pathway for electrons.

Minds On! In Lesson 2, you used wires to provide a path for electricity to flow. What other materials would make good paths for electric current? In your **Activity Log** on page 17, list some materials you think might work. ●

32

Cars move easily on a wide road.

EXPLORE Activity!

Will It Conduct?

You know that electricity is a flow of electrons. What kinds of things will permit a flow of electrons? Do some things allow electrons to flow better than other things?

What You Need

4 20-cm lengths of insulated copper wire
wire strippers or scissors
2 1.5-V cells and holders
2 light bulbs and holders
2 alligator clips

testable items:
12-cm length of copper pipe
glass rod
strip of aluminum foil 3 cm x 15 cm
wooden craft stick
rubber eraser
nail
brass screw
plastic pen cap
piece of pencil lead (graphite)
paper clip
diode (1N4001)
Activity Log pages 18–19

What To Do

Part A

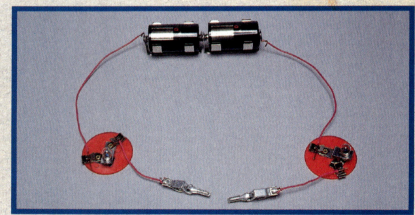

1 Set up a simple test circuit as shown. Use wire strippers or scissors carefully to scrape off about 1 cm of insulation at each end of each wire. Attach 2 wires to each of the bulb holders. Attach 1 wire from each of the bulb holders to 1 terminal of the battery. *Safety Tip:* Be careful working with sharp objects. Leave the other wire from each bulb holder unattached. Attach an alligator clip to each of the free ends of wire.

2 Before testing any objects, look at the objects and predict which ones will cause the bulbs to light. Write your predictions in your **Activity Log**.

See the *Safety Tip* in step 1.

34

3 Test the objects by attaching the alligator clips to each end of each object, one at a time. Does the object allow electrons to flow from the battery to the bulbs? How can you tell? Try reversing its direction. Does it affect the circuit?

4 In your *Activity Log*, use two columns. Label them "Bulbs light" or "closed circuit" and "Bulbs do not light" or "open circuit." As you test each item, record your observation in the correct column.

Part B

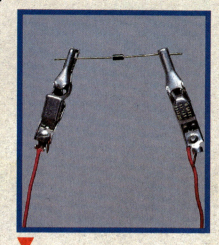

1 Use your test circuit again. This time, test a device called a diode. Place the diode as shown. Then turn it around. Does it matter which direction the current flows through the diode?

2 Are there other objects you would like to check? Predict whether you think they will make the bulbs light. Test the items to check your predictions.

3 Record your observations in your *Activity Log*.

What Happened?

1. Which of the objects allowed the bulbs to light?
2. Which of the objects didn't allow the bulbs to light?
3. Can you classify into one general group the objects that allowed the bulbs to light? What would that group be called?
4. Did the diode allow the bulbs to light? Explain your answer.

What Now?

1. Think about the electrical devices in your home and school. What do you think the wires attached to these devices are made of?
2. Why is it better to package a cell in plastic instead of aluminum foil?

EXPLORE

Four Kinds of Materials

In the Explore Activity on the previous two pages, you tested various objects to see which of them would allow the bulbs to light. Electricians call the circuit you made a **continuity** (kon´ tə nü´ i tē) **tester** because it tests for a continuous flow of electrons. You found the metal objects (the copper pipe, aluminum foil, nail, brass screw, and paper clip) allowed electrons to flow. These objects are conductors. **Conductors** are materials that permit electrons to move easily. Most, but not all, conductors are metals. For example, the nonmetallic substance called graphite (used in pencil lead) conducts electricity. Animal and plant tissues conduct electricity, too.

By using the continuity tester, you found some objects (the plastic pen cap, rubber eraser, and wooden craft stick) did not allow electrons to flow. We call such materials nonconductors, or insulators (in´ sə lā´ tərz). **Insulators** resist the movement of electrons. Insulators

A nail is a conductor.

are made of materials such as plastic, sulfur, rubber, glass, and wood. These materials won't allow electrons to flow.

We need conductors to allow electrons to flow. We use insulators to prevent electrons from flowing where we don't want them to. Think about the wires connecting your TV or radio to a plug. When you plug the TV into an outlet in the wall, you connect it to a circuit.

The wires running from TVs to plugs, from plugs to outlets, and from outlets to other places in a circuit are covered with an insulator. The insulator keeps you from receiving an electric shock whenever you plug in an electrical device, because insulators don't allow electricity to flow through them. For example, if the wires of your TV weren't insulated, electric current would go into your hand when you plugged in the TV. What would happen if wires inside a cord weren't insulated? Read the Health Link to find out.

A rubber eraser is an insulator.

Health Link

Fire From a Wire

You know electric current always flows in a closed circuit. Picture an iron plugged into an outlet in the wall. Inside the iron's cord are two wires. One wire carries the current from an outlet in the wall to the iron. The other wire returns current to the outlet. Inside the cord, each wire is surrounded by an insulator such as plastic. A second insulator surrounds both wires in the cord.

What if the insulation on the wires inside the cord wore away so the two wires touched each other? Remember that wire is a conductor. If the two wires touched, current would no longer flow all the way to the iron and then back along the circuit to the wall. Instead, the current would take a shorter route. It would flow to the place where the two wires touched and from there back to the outlet in the wall. When something like this happens, the wires heat up very quickly and could start a fire. If you're ever using an electrical appliance and the wires get hot, turn it off, unplug it, and take it to be repaired.

Removing the insulation from a wire can be hazardous.

Minds On! You know many words that begin with the prefix *semi-*: *semiattached, semisoft, semidesert,* etc. Think about what *semi-* means (partial or intermediate). Try to infer the meaning of *semiconductor.* ●

A **semiconductor** allows electricity to flow more easily than an insulator does, but not as easily as a conductor does. Think about the diode you used in your continuity tester. A diode is made from two types of semiconductors. Do you remember that the diode had to be facing a certain way in order for the bulb to light? A diode allows electricity to flow through it in only one direction, just as a one-way street allows traffic in only one direction or the valve in a vein allows blood to flow through it in only one direction. Diodes are found in many electrical devices where electricity can flow in just one direction. You'll learn about electricity that flows in one or two directions in Lesson 7.

Valves permit blood to flow only one way.

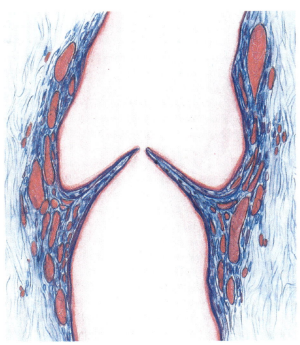

37

Focus on Technology

Conductors Without Resistance

You've learned about conductors, nonconductors (insulators), and semiconductors. What do you suppose a *superconductor* is? Is it most like a conductor, nonconductor, or semiconductor?

Sometimes we want electrical energy to be changed into heat. When we want to use electricity to produce heat, we design circuits to make electrons move through more resistance. But even when we don't want the electric current in a circuit to produce heat, some heat is produced anyway. Even the best conductors, such as copper wires, have some resistance to the flow of electrons. Whenever electrons must overcome resistance, they produce heat. The electrical energy that produces heat when we don't need heat is wasted energy.

During the 1950s, John Bardeen and two other physicists developed the first scientific theory to explain superconductivity. This team of physicists received the 1972 Nobel prize in physics.

Superconductors are materials that lose all of their resistance when they're cooled to a temperature near absolute zero (−273°C). So-called "high-temperature" superconductors lose most of their resistance when they are cooled to "only" −138°C! The big advantage of superconductors is that electrons flowing through them waste much less energy producing heat. Sending electricity over long distances (for example, from the power company to your home) would waste much less electrical energy as heat if superconductors could be used instead of regular wires.

What do you think is the disadvantage of a superconductor? The materials that can superconduct must be kept so cold it isn't practical to use them outside a laboratory. Can you imagine how cold it would be in your house if the wires in the walls had to be kept at a temperature below −200°C? Consider how much energy this would take!

Research scientists are experimenting to develop materials that can superconduct at room temperature. Some of their latest experiments involve superconducting materials made up of such complex mixtures of chemicals that they have been nicknamed "fruit salads."

At very low temperatures, superconductors have no resistance.

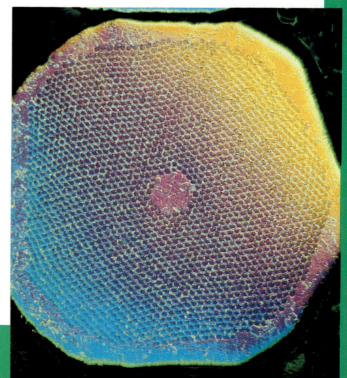

Conductors for Circuits

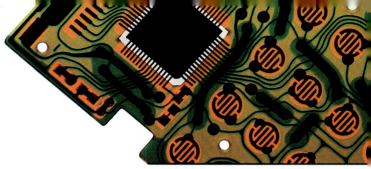

Many modern electrical devices, especially the small ones such as digital watches and pocket calculators, no longer use wires to carry electricity. Scientists and engineers have found cheaper and more efficient conducting paths for these devices. Look at the picture at the right. It shows a **printed circuit** from a computer. This circuit is contained on a piece of plastic. Trace the flow of electric current in the circuit. Notice the current doesn't flow through a wire. Instead, it uses metal pathways that were made by dipping the piece of plastic in a series of chemicals dissolved in water called "chemical baths."

Scientists have recently discovered they can make even smaller circuits. Edith Olson, a chemist with the United States Army, designed a way to shrink printed circuits. This design saved an estimated $200

Circuits can be printed onto a piece of plastic.

million a year. The amount of decrease in size of the printed circuits was compared to printing all the volumes in the Library of Congress on a grain of rice. Think about the size of the circuit that you made in Lesson 2. Then look at the electrical devices pictured on page 21. The circuits in these devices are much smaller than the circuit that you made! They are made on pieces of silicon crystals the size of sand grains. Thanks to these tiny circuits, engineers can make electrical devices and appliances smaller and smaller.

Do the activity below to see how objects can be coated with copper.

TRY THIS Activity!

A Coat of Copper

How would you like to try coating something with copper using a "chemical bath"?

What You Need
plastic cup, salt, vinegar, the circuit that you used to test whether materials will conduct, *Activity Log* page 20

Instead of connecting the copper wires to light bulbs, place them in an empty plastic or foam cup. Fill the cup about half full with vinegar. Add a spoonful of salt to the vinegar. Choose a key or similar metal object that you want to be coated with copper. Hang the object on the wire connected to the negative terminal of your battery. Drop both wires into the vinegar with salt. After 20 minutes, take the wires out of the liquid. What color has your object become? Write your observations in your *Activity Log*.

39

CAREERS

Electroplater

Conductors such as copper wires used in electric circuits need to be free from impurities such as sand that are insulators. One way of obtaining copper that is nearly 100 percent pure is to use a process known as electroplating. **Electroplating** deposits metal on the surface of a conductor. You did electroplating in the Try This Activity where you coated something with copper. A person who makes his or her living by doing electroplating is known as an **electroplater**.

An electroplater specializing in producing pure copper begins by obtaining impure copper ore from a copper mine or recycled copper materials that are full of impurities. The electroplater places the impure copper in a solution that contains a copper chemical dissolved in water. A small piece of pure copper is also placed in this solution. A source of electric current like a battery is then used to electroplate copper from the impure copper to the pure copper. The electroplater connects impure copper to the positive terminal of the battery and the pure copper to the negative battery terminal. More pure copper electroplates onto the piece of pure copper, making it larger and heavier. The impure copper becomes smaller and lighter in weight as it loses the copper in it. When the electroplater removes the source of electric current, a new piece of pure copper has been formed that can weigh many kilograms more than the original piece.

The pure copper produced by electroplaters can be changed into wires or other shapes. Electroplaters usually don't do this part of the job. They sell the pure copper to industries that manufacture copper into wires or other shapes. Many of the copper wires and electric circuits you've observed contain copper that was purified by an electroplater.

Electroplaters do not necessarily need a college degree. They learn their craft by practicing it. They must know a lot about different kinds of chemicals and about the ways in which electric current flows. Skilled electroplaters are able to electroplate many different metals onto nearly anything. Perhaps you've seen a pair of baby shoes that have been electroplated like the ones pictured. If you'd like to know more about electroplating, contact the American Electroplaters and Surface Finishers Society, 12644 Research Parkway, Orlando, FL 32826.

A skilled electroplater can electroplate almost anything.

Electroplaters serve a vital role in preparing conducting materials for electric circuits. Read the Literature Link to learn more about conductors of many kinds.

Literature  Link

Wires and Watts

"All common electrical wire is manufactured of copper and is covered with a nonconducting coating referred to as insulation... Wires used for appliance power cords, for example, may be covered with rubber or rubberlike material for flexibility, whereas those used within the walls of houses have heavy, nonflammable plastic coatings. Underground wires often have similar plastic insulation that is further enclosed in lead or other metallic outer jackets. Wires intended for high-temperature use are usually insulated with ceramic beads, while those intended for use under water have heavy rubber coatings."

In *Wires and Watts*, author Irwin Math describes wires you may have seen around your own home or school. Find some electrical wires and make a chart of their properties. Use a string or thread to measure each wire's diameter, and describe its insulation. Include the use for each wire and where it was found. **Safety Tip:** Examine electrical wires only with your eyes. Don't handle them. If you discover an unsafe wire, notify an adult to have it repaired.

Sum It Up

You've learned about four kinds of materials. A conductor is a material that allows the flow of electrons to occur easily. As you discovered in the Explore Activity on pages 34 and 35, metals are the most common conductors. Purified copper is the conductor used in most electric circuits. An insulator doesn't allow electrons to flow easily. Some common insulators are plastic, dry wood, and rubber. A semiconductor allows current to flow in it more easily than an insulator does, but not as easily as a conductor does. Superconductors are conductors with no resistance to the flow of electrons. Superconductors lose less electrical energy as heat than conductors do, but energy is needed to keep superconductors at very cold temperatures. In the next four lessons, you'll learn more about how these four kinds of materials are used in electric circuits.

Critical Thinking

1. People who repair electrical devices are careful to purchase plastic-handled tools. Why are plastic handles important?

2. In this unit, you've studied electrical insulators. People put insulation in a home to conserve heat or coolness. How are electrical insulators and heat insulators similar?

3. Why is it dangerous to use tap water (which conducts electricity) to put out a fire around electrical equipment? What should be used?

4. A car's body and many parts inside are made of metal. With all the electrical wires and equipment in a car, why aren't drivers and passengers shocked?

5. Most electrical appliances have many different colors and patterns on the wires. Why don't the makers use the same color on all the wires?

What's the Best Pathway for Electrons?

Picture two hikers who have come to a fork in the road. One takes the high road, and one takes the low road. Like those hikers, electrons can have more than one pathway in a circuit. This lesson looks at circuits with only one pathway for electrons and at circuits with two or more pathways.

Suppose you come up to bat in a game of baseball. You hit the ball into the outfield and run to first base. You're on your way to second base when an outfielder throws the ball to second base. The umpire yells, "Out!" You might say your movement around the bases was interrupted.

You know that electrons flow around a circuit in much the same way that players run around a baseball diamond. Think about a closed circuit that contains a light bulb, a battery, and conducting wires. What happens if there is only one pathway for the electrons to take and the flow of electrons around that pathway is interrupted? When that happens, the circuit is said to be broken. The light in the bulb goes off.

Imagine riding in a car on a two-lane, one-way street. The driver sees a stalled car ahead in your lane. He or she finds that the other lane is clear, moves the car over to that lane, and passes the stalled car. Because there was another pathway, your trip wasn't interrupted.

Minds On! Think of times when something interrupted the pathway you were taking, but you were able to keep moving because another pathway existed. Record these occasions in your ***Activity Log*** on page 21.●

A runner has just one pathway around the bases.

42

This runner's movement on the base path has been stopped.

43

EXPLORE Activity!

Find the Right Pathways!

You know a battery can push electrons in a circuit. When the battery is in a closed circuit, the electrons leave the negative end of the battery and flow through a conductor back to the positive end of the battery. In this activity, you'll explore some different pathways electrons can take from one end of a battery to the other.

What You Need

2 1.5-V cells with holders
2 light bulbs
2 bulb holders
voltmeter (0–3 V)
6 20-cm lengths of insulated copper wire
wire strippers or scissors
Activity Log pages 22–23

What To Do

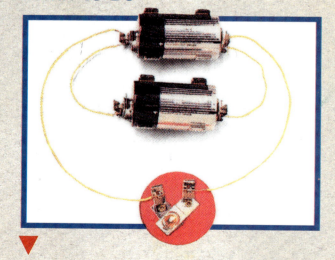

1 Set up Circuit A with both cells and 1 bulb as shown. Touch both screws on the bulb holder with the wires from the voltmeter. Record your observations in your *Activity Log*.

Now, remove 1 of the cells from the circuit. Touch both screws on the bulb holder again with the wires from the voltmeter. Record your observations.

2 Set up Circuit B with both cells and 1 bulb as shown. Test the bulb with the voltmeter. Record your observations. Now, remove 1 of the cells. Test the bulb with the voltmeter. Record your observations.

3 Set up Circuit C with both bulbs and 1 cell as shown. Test each bulb with the voltmeter. Record your observations in your *Activity Log*. Now, unscrew 1 of the bulbs. Test both bulbs with the voltmeter. Record your observations.

4 Set up Circuit D with both bulbs and 1 cell as shown. Test both bulbs with the voltmeter. Record your observations in your *Activity Log*. Now, unscrew 1 of the bulbs. Record your observations.

What Happened?

1. Which circuit produced the brightest light?
2. Which circuit had the highest voltmeter reading? The lowest voltmeter reading?
3. Which circuit didn't seem to be affected by removing a cell? By removing a bulb?

What Now?

1. What is an advantage of Circuit A? A disadvantage?
2. What is an advantage of Circuit B? A disadvantage?
3. What is an advantage of Circuit C? A disadvantage?
4. What is an advantage of Circuit D? A disadvantage?

EXPLORE

Designing Circuits

In the Explore Activity, you discovered that the flow of electrons is less likely to be interrupted in circuits with more than one pathway than in circuits with only one pathway. Circuits with more than one pathway for electrons to flow through are called **parallel circuits**. If one pathway is blocked, the electrons can flow through the other pathway or pathways. When one cell dies in a circuit with two cells connected in parallel, the other cell keeps the electrons flowing and the bulb will light.

Circuits with only one pathway for electrons to flow through are called **series circuits.** If this one pathway is blocked, electrons can no longer flow through the circuit. In a circuit with two cells connected in series, when one cell dies, the flow of electrons stops. The bulb will not light.

In a circuit that has two bulbs connected in parallel, when one bulb goes out, the other bulb will stay lit. But in a circuit that has two bulbs connected in series, when one bulb goes out, the other bulb won't stay lit. However, bulbs connected in series are not as bright as bulbs connected in parallel. Dimmer lights use less current. The battery lasts longer. Do the Try This Activity to investigate how batteries discharge differently in series and parallel.

Cells in parallel

Cells in series

Bulbs in parallel

Bulbs in series

TRY THIS

It Keeps Going and Going

You can use motors to investigate how connecting two batteries in series or in parallel will cause them to discharge at a different rate.

What You Need
2 1.5-volt motors
2 1.5-volt cells set up in parallel as on page 44
2 1.5-volt cells set up in series as on page 45
Activity Log page 24

Connect the parallel and series cells to the motors. Make a hypothesis about which cells will discharge first. Over the course of the school day, observe and record in your *Activity Log* what is happening to the motors. If the motors are still running at the end of the school day disconnect them from the cells. At the start of the next day connect both motors at the same time. Which cells discharged first? Was your hypothesis correct? Write an explanation as to what caused the cells to discharge at a different rate in your *Activity Log.*

Do all the electric devices in your home go off if one goes off? No. How inconvenient it would be if every time you turned off the television set, all the electrical appliances in your home went off, too! To prevent this, parallel circuits instead of series circuits are used in homes.

Think about the baseball play described at the beginning of this lesson. What kind of circuit, series or parallel, does a baseball diamond resemble? Players running the bases must touch each base before advancing. In the same way, electrons must flow through each element in a series circuit. Just as there's only one pathway for baseball players, in a series circuit there's only one pathway for electrons.

By contrast, a parallel circuit provides more than one pathway. Think about a car changing lanes to pass a stalled car. The moving car is able to continue on a parallel pathway (the other lane). When elements in a circuit are in parallel, the electrons can flow around disconnected elements and continue flowing through the circuit. If a battery dies or a bulb burns out, electrons can follow a different path to the next element in the circuit. We use parallel circuits when it's important to keep everything from going off all at once.

Today, the use of series circuits is usually limited to simple devices, such as flashlights and holiday lights. Have you ever replaced the batteries in a flashlight? If so, you may know that most flashlights and other battery-powered devices use more than one cell placed in series. Why? Using more than one cell connected in series increases the voltage. According to Ohm's Law, increasing the voltage of a circuit also increases the current.

Increasing the current in a flash-light means the bulb will burn brighter, but the cells won't last as long. Cells in parallel act as two separate cells. Therefore it takes longer for the cells to be used up.

Series circuits are also used for devices that require all the parts to be affected when one part is disconnected. A security system, for example, uses a series circuit. When an intruder causes a break anywhere in the circuit, the flow of electrons is interrupted and the alarm is tripped.

Most electrical devices have printed on them the number of cells they need. You install the cells in a flashlight top to bottom (positive end to negative end). For a battery with cells connected in series, you can calculate total voltage by adding the voltages of all the cells.

Many flashlights use two cells in series.

Automobile Electrical Systems

The electrical system of a gasoline-powered car combines series and parallel circuits. The battery of a typical car consists of six 2-volt cells connected in series to produce 12 volts. The electrical devices in a car operate on 12 volts.

One 12-volt battery is very useful for starting a gasoline engine, but one 12-volt battery wouldn't take a car very far if it was the only source of energy. Have you ever ridden in a vehicle that had no engine but used batteries as its source of energy? Do the Math Link to learn more about using batteries to run a car.

Two vehicles are approaching you at night. Both vehicles have only one headlight. One of them is a car, and the other is a motorcycle. The car has lost the use of one headlight. What do you think is true about the light circuit in a car?

Math Link

This Car Runs on Batteries, Not Gasoline

In this lesson, you used a miniature motor that was powered by two 1.5-volt cells. You observed that using two of these cells connected in series made the motor move faster. Suppose the motors were being used to operate a toy car. This toy car would move faster using two cells than it would with one cell. Remember the relationship between potential, current, and resistance known as Ohm's Law: amps = volts ÷ ohms. Ohm's Law predicts that connecting cells or batteries in series will increase the voltage and the current. This makes the motor move faster.

Have you ever ridden in an electric car?

Now, suppose a car had a motor that ran on 220 volts, as many electric motors do. How many 12-volt batteries would need to be connected in series in order to supply 220 volts?

**Number of batteries =
220 volts ÷ 12 volts per battery
Number of batteries = ?**

Draw a diagram in your ***Activity Log*** on page 25 that includes eighteen 12-volt batteries connected in series. Compare your diagram with those drawn by your classmates. Think of a name for each car that would use the array of batteries in each diagram. For example, a car with all eighteen batteries in a straight line might be called the *Plankmobile*.

Write each name and copy each diagram in your ***Activity Log*** on page 25.

One morning you see a parked car with its headlights on. It's easy to forget to turn off your headlights on mornings when you set out in the dark but arrive in daylight. On such mornings, the driver may forget that the lights are on. What problem could arise if the lights remain on for several hours?

The headlights are connected in parallel. Parallel lights give brighter light than series lights. A parallel connection also lets one light keep shining if the other goes out. Lights won't cause a car's battery to discharge totally as long as the car is running. Cars are equipped with generators that recharge the battery while the engine is running. (You'll learn more about how generators work in Lesson 7.) If the lights are left on after the engine is stopped, the battery will soon discharge. You observed how lights can drain a battery when you did the Explore Activity.

Sum It Up

Electrical systems make use of series circuits and parallel circuits or a combination of these two. Series circuits are designed so that the electricity flows through all parts of the circuit in one pathway. Series circuits are used in special situations and are mostly seen in simple devices such as flashlights and security systems. For example, flashlight cells connected in series give a brighter light. Parallel circuits provide alternate paths for current to flow through. Parallel circuits are widely used because they prevent overall electrical failure should one element in the circuit fail.

Knowing how a series and parallel pathway affects a current helps you understand how to use electrical energy safely and effectively. In the next lesson, you'll learn more about familiar circuits that combine elements in series and parallel.

Critical Thinking

1. When sources of electricity are added in series, you add their voltages to get the total voltage. An automobile battery is actually a set of several smaller batteries called cells. The cells are connected in series side by side. If each cell in an automobile battery produces 2.1 volts (Note: this is different from regular 1.5-volt dry cells), then what's the total voltage of an automobile battery with three cells? With six cells?

2. Some police officers like to use long flashlights that hold five batteries. What's the total voltage in the flashlight? Why would using five batteries be good?

3. It's not unusual to see a car with two horns. Is one horn connected in series or parallel with the other horn? How could you find out?

4. Some strings of holiday lights come equipped with flashers. The flasher opens and closes the light circuit as the metal in it heats and cools. The flasher makes the lights blink on and off. Is the flasher connected in series or in parallel? How do you know?

5. You've been given five batteries, some wire, and a bulb. Your challenge: to build a flashlight that will burn as long as possible. What kind of circuit will you use? Explain.

How Can You Stop the Flow of Electricity?

The current stops with a flick of the wrist. The current starts with a simple twist. In this lesson, you'll identify several devices used to open and close a circuit.

What do you suppose happens to the flow of electrons when you turn on the light in your bathroom? What do you suppose happens to the flow of electrons when you turn it off? Which action would make an open circuit? Which would make a closed circuit? Think about what you already know about electric circuits and the way electrons flow through them to light a bulb.

Suppose you're trying to be helpful in the morning. You turn on the toaster, waffle iron, radio, and electric juicer all at once. Chances are, the circuit would be overloaded. Have you ever overloaded a circuit? Then the toaster, waffle iron, radio, and juicer suddenly stop working. What do you do?

Mind's On! What if all the electrical appliances in in your home couldn't be turned off? What might happen to the appliances and to your family? Imagine the noise, confusion, and danger that would result. Write three or four sentences in your ***Activity Log*** on page 26 describing such a scene. ●

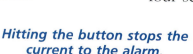

Hitting the button stops the current to the alarm.

50

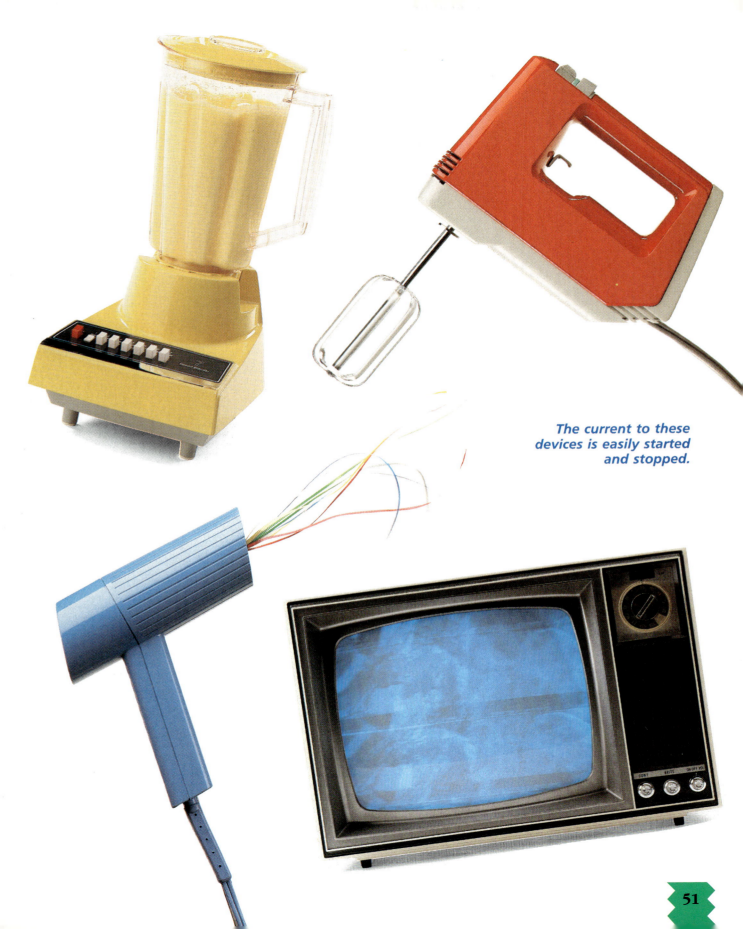

The current to these devices is easily started and stopped.

EXPLORE Activity!

Stopping the Flow

Which of the materials you tested on pages 34 and 35 were conductors? You know how to get electrons to flow in a conductor by connecting the conductor to an open place in the circuit. Is there an easier way to get electrons to start and to stop flowing in a conductor?

What You Need

2 bulbs/holders
1.5-V cell/holder
5 30-cm lengths of insulated copper wire
aluminum (foil or pie plates)
masking tape
2 brass paper fasteners
2 paper clips
2 wooden clothespins
scissors
piece of cardboard 25 cm x 25 cm
Activity Log pages 27–28

What To Do

1. Set up a circuit with 1 cell, 2 bulbs, and 5 wires. Invent a device that will allow you to turn each light bulb off and on in the circuit. To do this, you must build a new device into the circuit. This device will allow you to move something to turn the circuit off and on. Everything that you will need to invent your device is available at the supply table. *Safety Tip:* Observe caution when working with sharp objects.

2. After you have built your device into the circuit, draw a diagram of your setup in your *Activity Log*. Demonstrate how this device allows you to turn each light bulb off and on. Observe as others demonstrate the devices they invented. Save your device for the activity in Lesson 6.

See the *Safety Tip* in step 1.

52

Use these materials to invent your device that turns a circuit on and off.

What Happened?
1. What did your device do to the flow of electrons through the circuit?
2. How did it do this?
3. Compare your device to those developed by others. What do they have in common?

What Now?
1. The device you made is called a switch. What are some of the electrical devices you have at home that have switches? List these devices in your **Activity Log**.
2. Give an example of a place in your home or community that has two or more electrical devices on the same switch.
3. What must be true about two or more electrical devices that can be controlled by the same switch?

EXPLORE

53

Safely On and Off

In the Explore Activity, you built a switch. A switch controls the flow of electrons in a circuit. When a switch is on, the electric circuit is complete or closed, and electrons can flow through the circuit. When a switch is off, the electric circuit is incomplete or open, and electrons can't flow through the circuit.

You know switches are used on almost all electrical appliances. We need switches for convenience. Think how awkward it would be to have to pull a plug every time you wanted to turn off a lamp! We also need switches for safety. Some big switches allow us to turn off all the electrical power in a house. Being able to turn off all the electrical power is essential in case of fire.

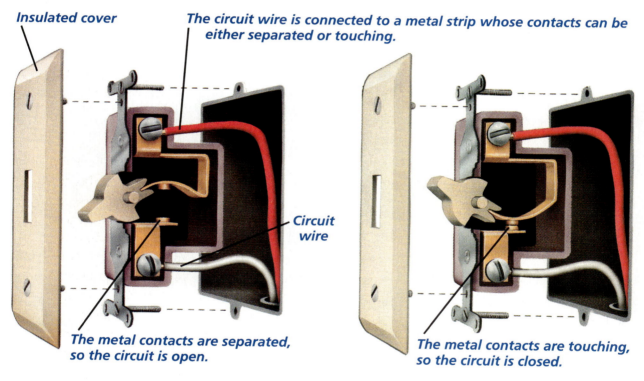

Insulated cover

The circuit wire is connected to a metal strip whose contacts can be either separated or touching.

Circuit wire

The metal contacts are separated, so the circuit is open.

The switch is in the off position.

The metal contacts are touching, so the circuit is closed.

The switch is in the on position.

Minds On! Not all switches are alike. Think about switches on appliances and devices and on the walls of your home. What do these switches look like? What do they do? How do you make them work? In your **Activity Log** on page 29, list some of the ways in which switches are alike and different. ●

Because this switch is connected in series with the bulb and the cells, the bulb will light when the circuit is closed.

The switch opens and closes the circuit.

Because this switch is connected in parallel with the bulb and cells, the bulb won't light. There is a short circuit.

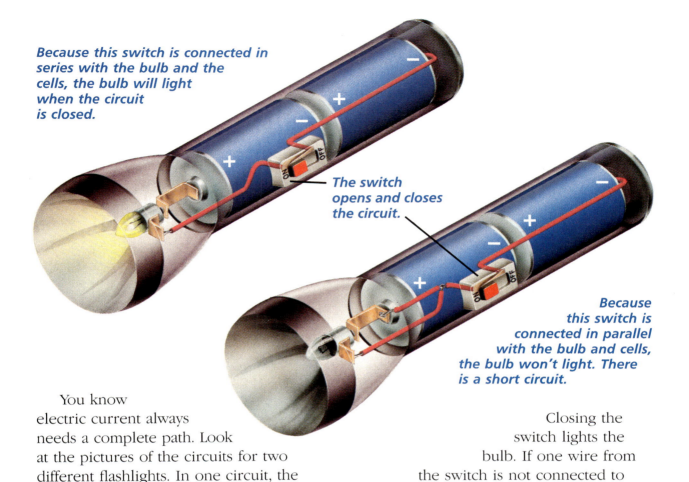

You know electric current always needs a complete path. Look at the pictures of the circuits for two different flashlights. In one circuit, the wires from the switch are connected to the positive end of one cell and to the negative end of the other cell. In the other circuit, one wire from the switch is connected to the bulb instead of the cell.

In Lesson 4, you learned about series and parallel circuits. In the Explore Activity on pages 52 and 53, you built a switch into a circuit. Before answering the question that follows, think back about how you constructed and used your switch.

Here's the question: Must a switch be wired in series or parallel with what it is to control? Why?

When the wires from the switch are connected to the bulb and the negative end of one cell, the switch is in series with the bulb in the electric circuit of the flashlight.

Closing the switch lights the bulb. If one wire from the switch is not connected to the bulb, the bulb won't light when the switch is closed. Instead the wires become warm, and the cells are quickly discharged due to a larger current. When something like this happens, you have a short circuit. According to Ohm's Law, the current in a **short circuit** is larger because the resistance is smaller. The wires heat up very quickly. If the current isn't interrupted, it can start a fire. In the Health Link on page 37, you learned that you have to disconnect an electrical device when you notice the wires becoming warm. Even devices controlled by a switch should be disconnected from a battery or an outlet in the case of a short circuit. Disconnecting the device prevents it from being switched on again by someone who doesn't know about the short circuit.

You know a circuit can overheat if a short circuit is created. A circuit can also overheat if too many electrical appliances wired in parallel are turned on at the same time. This causes more current in the circuit. The pictures on this page show two types of switches known as fuses and circuit breakers. **Fuses** and **circuit breakers** are types of switches that operate by themselves.

Remember how you built your switch to be in series with each bulb? Fuses and circuit breakers are built into circuits in just the same way. These switches interrupt the flow of electrons when a circuit has too much current in it. Every building should have fuses or circuit breakers to interrupt, or open, the circuit before the current can become great enough to start a fire or damage electrical devices. Perhaps you've noticed electrical outlets that have small reset buttons. These buttons are part of a circuit breaker known as a Ground Fault Circuit Interrupter (GFCI). A GFCI prevents electric shocks by opening a circuit when a defective device is plugged in.

Once a fuse melts, it must be replaced. By contrast, a circuit breaker can simply be reset to the *on* position once the problem that caused the overload has been solved. Why might you prefer circuit breakers to fuses? To become better acquainted with fuses and circuit breakers, do the Try This Activity below.

Circuit breakers can be reset.

When too much current blows a fuse, the fuse must be replaced.

Although your body doesn't have a service panel that would permit you or a physician to check the circuit breakers when something is wrong, your body does have ways of preventing damage to vital organs in your body. Read the Health Link on the next page to learn about one way your body prevents damage to your brain.

TRY THIS Activity!

Observe Your Service Panel

What You Need
circuit-breaker service panel
adult
***Activity Log* page 30**

You can learn how circuit breakers are used. Have an adult show you the circuit-breaker service panel in your home or in a community building. Ask for instructions on how to reset a circuit breaker that has been opened. Draw a diagram in your *Activity Log* of this service panel including the name of each circuit as it is marked on the panel. Bring this diagram to class to compare with your classmates' diagrams.

Preventing a Drain on Your Brain

You know that circuit breakers interrupt the flow of electrons when a circuit is overloaded. Your body behaves as if it had a circuit breaker when you faint. How? Imagine you're outside watching a baseball game and you're standing because all of the seats are taken. You become dizzy, but you must keep standing without any seats available. You see the ball, but you can't tell which team has just hit a home run. Somebody tells you the home run was hit by your team. You want to cheer. Instead you faint.

You might be angry at yourself or embarrassed if that were to happen. But fainting is a protective mechanism, like a circuit breaker.

You know to check electrical devices for worn insulation before plugging them in. Worn insulation is a warning sign that a short circuit could occur. In the same way, you should pay attention to the warning signs of fainting. These signs include weakness, dizziness, headaches, and mental confusion. If you feel that you're about to faint, sometimes you can prevent it by positioning your head lower than your heart. For example, you might lie down and elevate your feet.

Sometimes fainting occurs despite our efforts to heed the warning signs. Do library research to find out what to do if someone faints. Also find out what kind of activities are likely to cause a person to faint. Then, working in groups of two or three, make a poster titled *"What To Do Before and After Someone Faints."* Display it and discuss it with your classmates.

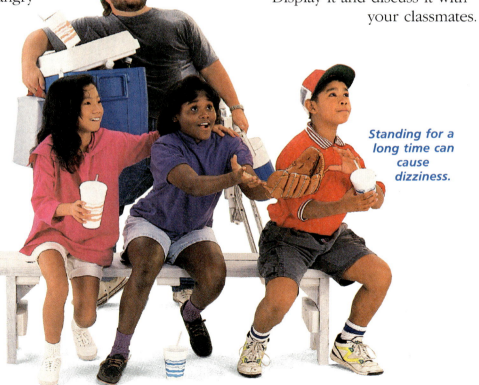

Standing for a long time can cause dizziness.

A Much-needed Break

Rather than buying new fuses, some people replace burned-out fuses with pennies. How do pennies and fuses compare in thickness? Which one would permit more current to flow? Think about what purpose a fuse serves. Why do you think it's very dangerous to replace a burned-out fuse with a penny?

Minds On! Look at the picture of the chain made of colored yarn. Think about the links in a chain. Assume some links are weaker than others. Suppose you hold one end of the chain and your friend holds the other. You and your friend exert forces on either end of the chain. If the chain breaks, at what point will it break? Describe how the weak link in the chain works like a fuse in a circuit. Write your explanation in your **Activity Log** on page 31.

Some household electrical appliances and devices have their own built-in circuit breakers. These protect them from sudden surges, or unexpected large amounts of current electricity. Some clothes irons and space heaters even have circuit breakers that turn off these devices if they tip over. Examine the back of your television set. You'll probably find a red circuit breaker. When people call a TV repairperson to complain about a problem in their set, she or he might tell them to reset the circuit breaker. If the circuit breaker was tripped because of a momentary power surge, this often solves the problem.

If you pull the chain too hard, what will happen?

58

Sum It Up

One way to control the flow of electrons in a circuit is by using a switch. You invented a simple switch in the Explore Activity on pages 52 and 53. The main purpose of a simple switch is to provide a means to open and close a circuit. Fuses and circuit breakers are two kinds of switches. Both interrupt the flow of electrons when a circuit is overloaded. They are safety features used in many electrical systems. Fuses, circuit breakers, and other kinds of switches allow us to use electrical energy safely in devices found in our community.

Critical Thinking

1. Franklin is at home alone when one of the fuses in his home burns out. He goes to the fuse box and sees that a 20-amp fuse has burned out. The only spare fuse he can find is a 30-amp fuse. Would it be dangerous for him to use it as a replacement? Explain what he should do.

2. Suppose the turn signals on an automobile stop working. You check the control panel of the automobile and discover that a 20-amp fuse labeled "turn signals" is out. You replace the fuse with another 20-amp fuse. This fuse quickly goes out, too. Should you replace the 20-amp fuse with a fuse of larger size? Why or why not?

3. You are sitting in the living room at a friend's house. There are two ceiling lamps, and plugged into wall outlets are a floor lamp, a tape player, and a fan. Suddenly, the two ceiling lamps go out, though no one has switched them off. The other three appliances stay turned on. Provide two explanations for this occurrence. Which explanation is the more probable? What should your friend do to solve the problem?

4. Depending on how you look at it, you could say that a fuse is hooked up in parallel or in series. How can this be?

5. Most homes have a main breaker switch somewhere outside the house. Using this switch, all the electric power to a house can be turned off at once. Why is a main breaker switch necessary? Is the main breaker switch connected in series or in parallel?

How Are Electricity and Magnetism Related?

Magnetism is more than a magnet sticking to a piece of steel. A knowledge of magnetism will help you understand how many electrical devices work. When you see how magnetism is related to electricity, you'll realize why electricity and magnetism are studied together.

Look at the picture on this page. What does this doorbell have in common with a stereo speaker, telephone, and compass? All these devices, and many more besides, use magnets to do work. Remember that a magnet is any object that can exert a force on iron or steel without touching it. How do magnets aid these devices in doing work? Some use electricity to make magnets do the work. What do you think the relationship is between the electricity running through these devices and the magnets in these devices?

The words *electricity* and *magnetism* come from Greek words. Unlike *electricity,* which comes from the Greek word *elektron* meaning "amber," magnetism comes from the name of an area in Greece (*Magnesia*). Magnets were first discovered in Magnesia where people noticed metals were attracted to lodestones.

Minds On! What other words can you think of that come from Greek words? Write these words in your **Activity Log** on page 32. Compare your list with the lists of your classmates. ●

A doorbell is one of many devices that uses a magnet to cause motion.

60

It Opened the World

"It is well to observe the force and virtue and consequence of discoveries. These are to be seen nowhere more conspicuously than in those three [discoveries] which were unknown to the ancients...namely, printing, gunpowder, and the magnet (that is, the magnetic compass). For these three have changed the whole face and state of things throughout the world."

Francis Bacon
English philosopher
1561–1626

Have you ever used a compass like the one pictured on this page? A compass comes in handy if you go hiking or sailing. It can help you navigate, or find your way, in the woods or on the sea. Notice that the compass pictured has a needle inside it. The needle is a magnet.

The compass was invented over 1,000 years ago in China. At first, Chinese sailors used compasses to find their way back home when they went out gathering a precious green stone called jade. Perhaps you have seen pieces of jewelry made of jade.

By the year A.D. 1117, the Chinese had started using the compass for navigation. A book written in that year reported, "The pilots who steered the ships knew the shape of the coasts; at night they steer by the stars, and in the daytime by the sun. In dark weather they look at the...[compass] needle." Before the compass, ship pilots could only navigate in clear weather and within sight of the shoreline.

Over the next 100 years, knowledge of the compass spread from China to Arabia and from Arabia to Europe. Soon Arabs and Europeans were using the compass for navigation. The compass had a tremendous impact on the world. With the compass, sailors could venture far away from land and still be sure of finding their way back home. They could navigate in cloudy or foggy weather. So sailors sailed to many new countries. People who lived very far from each other began to trade goods, knowledge, and skills. For example, people in Europe traveled by sea to trade with people in India and Africa.

The ancients found natural magnets to magnetize the needles in their compasses. Do the following activity to explore how magnets are made today.

The needle in a compass is a magnet.

61

EXPLORE Activity!

Making Electromagnets!

Can you use electricity to make any object magnetic? Can you make magnetism come and go? How do you make a stronger magnet? This activity helps you to answer these questions.

What You Need

sandpaper
60–100-cm length of insulated copper wire
pencil
compass
your switch from Lesson 5
2 1.5-V cells/holders
iron nail
7.5-cm bolt
box of small paper clips
Activity Log pages 33–34

What To Do

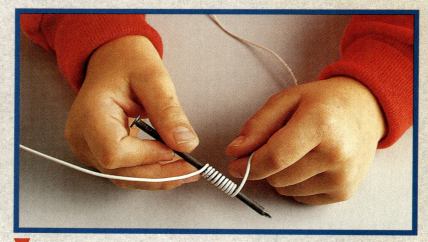

1. Construct a wire-coiled nail as shown. Wind the copper wire around the nail 10 times. Be sure the loops of wire do not overlap but are very close together. Leave 10–15 cm of either end of the wire uncoiled. **Safety Tip:** Be careful working with sharp objects.

2. With the switch open, attach the coil to the battery. Test the coil with a compass.

3. Bend 1 paper clip to form a hook. Close the switch, test the coiled nail with a compass, and try to pick up the hook. Open the switch after 5 seconds. Write your observations in your **Activity Log**.

See the *Safety Tip* in step 1.

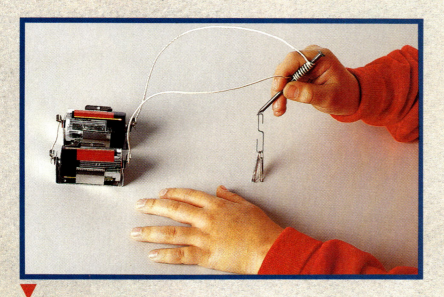

4 How many paper clips can you pick up with your nail? Close the switch and add paper clips one at a time to the hook. Open the switch when the nail drops the paper clips. Record this number in a table in your *Activity Log.*

5 Now, add 10 more loops of wire around the nail. Repeat steps 3 and 4.

6 Repeat step 5 once more.

7 Unwrap the wire from the nail. Repeat steps 1–6 using a pencil instead of a nail.

8 Unwrap the wire from the pencil. Repeat steps 1–6 using a bolt instead of a nail.

What Happened?

1. What number of loops allowed the nail to pick up the most paper clips? Why do you think this is so?
2. How did the pencil and the bolt compare with the nail?

What Now?

1. If you open the switch, does the nail, pencil, or bolt continue to pick up paper clips? Explain.
2. How do the magnets you constructed compare with other magnets you've seen?
3. Construct the strongest electromagnet you can.

EXPLORE

Magnetism With and Without Wires

In the Explore Activity, you used electricity to make a temporary magnet. When you closed the switch, electrons flowed through the wire that was wrapped, or coiled, around the nail. Whenever electric current passes through a wire, a magnetic field is created. A **magnetic field** exerts forces on surrounding iron and steel objects. When electricity flowed through the coils, the magnetic field of the coils of wire exerted forces on the nail, and the nail became an **electromagnet**.

Why is an electromagnet a "temporary" magnet? Think about the nail picking up paper clips. When the switch was on, current passed through the wire coils, and the nail became an electromagnet. Then you could use it to pick up paper clips. But after the nail had been removed from the electric current, it lost most of its magnetic properties.

You made your electromagnet stronger by wrapping more coils of wire around the nail. Each loop of wire also strengthened the magnetic field around the magnet. The more coils of wire you used, the more paper clips the nail could pick up. The more coils used in any electromagnet, the stronger the electromagnet is. You can also increase the strength of the electromagnet—and that of the magnetic field—by passing more current through the coils.

A huge electromagnet, attached to a crane, lifts scrap metal in a junkyard. Think about how many coils of wire are needed to make an electromagnet that size! The electromagnet on the crane works just like

Opening the switch will cause this electromagnet to lose most of its magnetic properties.

the one you made. When someone switches the current on, the electromagnet can pick up tons of scrap metal. When the current is switched off, the iron core of the electromagnet loses its magnetism. The scrap metal falls.

You've learned how electricity can be used to make a magnet. In the next lesson, you'll use a magnet to make electricity. You're probably beginning to realize that magnetism and electricity are related to each other. Think about the electromagnet you made. You know that when the switch was on and current passed through the wire, a magnetic field was created. The nail was positioned inside the magnetic field. What effect did the magnetic field have on the nail?

Objects such as nails and bolts that contain iron can be magnetized. They have atoms that act like tiny permanent magnets. A **domain** is a region where a group of neighboring atomic magnets point in the same direction. Usually, the different domains aren't pointing in the same direction but point in all directions. A whole nail will not become a magnet unless all its magnetic domains are pointing in the same direction. Starting a current in a wire looped around a nail will cause the magnetic domains to point in the direction of the magnetic field surrounding the wire. Stopping the current stops the magnetic field, and the magnetic domains in the nail go back to being pointed in all directions.

Do the following activity to observe magnetic fields.

TRY THIS Activity!

Observing Magnetic Fields

You've discovered that electric charges will attract or repel each other. What do you suppose the poles of a magnet do? It's possible to observe the region surrounding a magnet and whether the poles are attracting or repelling.

What You Need

self-sealing plastic bag containing iron filings, 2 bar magnets, goggles, *Activity Log* page 35

Safety Tip: Wear goggles to perform this activity. Place one of the magnets on the table. Lay the bag of iron filings, spread flat, over the middle of the magnet.

Watch the filings form a pattern. In your *Activity Log,* draw the pattern you see. Mark the ends of your drawing with **N** or **S** to indicate the north or south poles of the magnet.

Now place 2 magnets on the table with like poles near and parallel to each other about 1 or 2 cm apart. Have the south ends both facing to the right. Lay the bag of iron filings over the magnets.

Draw the pattern you see in your *Activity Log.* Be sure to label the poles.

Next, remove the bag of iron filings. Move the 2 magnets to make 1 north and 1 south end face right. Replace the bag of iron filings on top of the magnets. Draw the pattern in your *Activity Log.*

65

Think about the activity you just did with the magnets and the iron filings. The patterns the magnets created with the iron filings show the magnets' magnetic fields, which otherwise would be invisible. You worked as a scientist in this activity. As a scientist, you had to make observations of something that you couldn't see—the force lines of magnetic fields. To do this, you used something you could see—the iron filings—as a marker. Scientists often use the same technique. When they make observations of the flow of air, which they can't see, scientists use something that they can see—smoke or dust—as a marker.

Think about each of the patterns you drew in your **Activity Log** on page 35. When you worked with just one magnet, you saw lines radiating out from each pole and some lines running from north to south. In your first drawing, the iron filings were clustered around the poles. What do you think this means? The clustering of the lines shows that the magnetic field is strongest at the poles of a magnet.

During their early investigations of magnets, Chinese scientists discovered that Earth itself acts like a huge bar magnet. Where is Earth's magnetic field strongest? The north and south poles of Earth's magnetic field are located very near Earth's geographic North and South Poles.

Look back at the compass pictured on page 61. Notice the letter **N** stamped on one end of the needle. One end of a compass needle points toward Earth's north magnetic pole. We say a compass needle "seeks" the north pole. Do you think the magnetic pole near the North Pole is a "north" magnetic pole or a "south" magnetic pole? **1**

Look at the third drawing you made. When the poles of the magnets faced in opposite directions, the lines of force from their magnetic fields ran together. Opposite poles attract. In the second drawing, when the poles of the magnets faced in the same direction, the force lines of their magnetic fields pushed each other away because like poles repel.

Read the following page on using compasses to find out how people use magnetism for navigation.

This compass needle is pointing away from the magnet's north pole.

Bar magnet viewed from above.

The lines of magnetic force are invisible.

This compass needle is pointing toward the magnet's south pole.

The needle of a compass seeks the south pole of a bar magnet.

Social Studies Link
Setting a Compass

You already know you can use a compass to find your way. You know a compass needle points to the magnetic north pole. But did you know that to navigate with a compass, you must first set the compass so that it points to "true north?" That is, the needle must seek the geographic North Pole.

Look at the map of Earth on this page. The map is like a compass. The lines running north to south trace a path from places on Earth to the magnetic poles. The map also gives information you can use to adjust the paths so that they lead to the geographic North Pole.

Notice the measurements on the lines. They tell how many degrees east or west you would have to adjust your compass to travel to the geographic or true north. This measurement is called the **declination** (dek´ lə nā´ shən). As you can see, the declination varies depending where on Earth you are.

If you know the declination of the place you are going, it is possible to set a compass so it points true north. Some compasses permit you simply to turn a screw, shifting the position of the numbers on the compass housing until the end of the needle stamped **N** points the same number of degrees east or west as the declination.

Working in groups of four, choose four places on the map that you would like to visit. Use the map to find the declination for each place, so you can set your compass and not get lost. Make a class chart or a poster. Have each group write the names of the places they chose and their declinations. Show your classmates how to set a compass for each location.

Earth's magnetic poles and geographic poles are in different locations.

Declination lines tell you how much to adjust your compass.

A dolphin may have a natural compass in its head.

Humans aren't the only species to use magnetism for navigation. Pigeons, dolphins, and some sea turtles have particles of magnetite in their heads that may act as compasses. Magnetite is a mineral containing iron. It is possible that the particles of magnetite acting as compasses help these animals guide themselves.

For hundreds of years, scientists all over the world hypothesized that electricity and magnetism were related. But the relationship wasn't understood until 1820, when a Danish scientist named Hans Christian Oersted accidentally placed a compass under a wire that at the time was carrying electric current. What do you suppose Oersted observed? The compass needle moved.

Remember, a compass needle is a magnet. When the needle moved, Oersted knew the electric current had produced a magnetic field around it. His experiment proved that electricity and magnetism are related. You demonstrated this relationship yourself when you used electricity to produce a magnetic field. You sent an electric current through coils of wire that were wrapped around a nail, and the nail became a magnet.

Several years after Oersted's experiment, an English scientist named Michael Faraday pushed a strong magnet inside a coil of copper wire. Then he moved the magnet back and forth in the coil. As Faraday moved the magnet into the wire coil, the electrons in the coil also started to move. A small electric current was produced. In Lesson 7, you'll learn about a very important device that Faraday's experiment made possible: the electric generator. But before you're introduced to the generator, do the following activity to observe what Faraday discovered.

TRY THIS Activity!

A Magnetic Current

Can a magnet cause an electric current? Try this activity to find out.

What You Need

100-cm length of insulated copper wire, bar magnet, compass, Activity Log page 36

Wrap 20 coils of wire around the magnet. Join the two ends of the wire together. Hold a compass over the joined wires. Move the magnet back and forth in the loops of wire. Record your observations of the compass needle's movements in your **Activity Log**.

Shh! There Are Magnets in Here!

You know that many of the devices you see every day, such as doorbells and telephones, use magnets to do work. But did you know that audiocassette players and videocassette recorders (VCRs) use magnets, too?

The tapes in these devices are made of a plastic material that contains bits of iron. When music, voices, or pictures are recorded, the recorder lines up the magnetic particles in different ways that represent a code. Cassette players and VCRs interpret the code and translate it into electronic signals and then into sounds or pictures.

Because video and music cassettes store information in magnetic messages, they must be kept away from magnets. Bringing a strong magnet toward a cassette will cause the magnetic domains on the tape to line up in the magnetic field. The message on the tape will probably be erased! Try it with a tape you plan to erase.

The widespread use of electronic devices like VCRs and TVs has led to many career opportunities. Read the following Career article to learn more about one of these careers.

CAREERS

Electronic Service Technician

Suppose you turn on the television set and see crisscrossed lines instead of pictures. You fiddle with the antenna, but still no picture appears on the screen. What do you do? You call a repairperson or television service technician.

People who repair television sets can also repair VCRs, radios, stereo headsets, public-address systems, and many other electronic devices. Sometimes these technicians do a kind of detective work to locate the source of a problem, checking the circuits with instruments such as voltmeters, ammeters, and oscilloscopes. Of course, once they locate the problem, they must know how to fix it!

If you decided to become a TV repairperson, you would attend a technical school for one or two years. You know that magnetism and electricity make TVs and other electronic devices possible. In addition to learning more about electricity and magnetism, you would be trained in working with electronic devices. After graduation, you would spend several years in on-the-job training to become a fully-qualified service technician.

Audio and video tapes contain magnetic domains.

SCIENCE TECHNOLOGY AND Society

Focus on Technology

Electronic Surveillance

Have you ever been shopping and glimpsed yourself on a television screen in the store? If you have, then you've experienced electronic surveillance. Electronic surveillance (sər vā´ ləns) is the use of electronic devices like video cameras and tape recorders to make observations and obtain evidence. The use of electronic surveillance has become widespread throughout the world.

Does electronic surveillance help to reduce crime and catch criminals? Many lawbreakers are in prison today because they committed a crime while a video camera recorded them. However, some people who plan crimes are no longer overlooking the presence of a video camera. They make plans for the camera to be disconnected or for it to be looking the other way when performing a robbery. When this happens, not only does a store owner lose the stolen items, but even the cost of operating a video camera becomes a loss. To make up for these losses, customers pay higher prices for goods.

If the use of electronic surveillance reduces crime, shouldn't there be less crime now than there was 10 or 20 years ago? Statistics from law enforcement agencies indicate that the crime rate has increased more than the rate of population growth. This includes the crime rate for major felonies like armed robbery. Many businesses have invested in electronic surveillance equipment hoping to discourage attempted robberies. Although this equipment can discourage possible thieves from attempting crimes they know will be filmed, it also can cause law-abiding citizens to feel their privacy is being invaded. Shoppers may choose to shop in a store where they know they're not being watched.

Suppose you own a business that does not presently use electronic surveillance. Would you install the equipment? Where would you install it to avoid offending your customers? How would you prevent a potential thief from disconnecting it or in some other way defeating it? Write your ideas in a short essay in your **Activity Log** on page 37.

Have you been on TV?

You know the less resistance there is in a circuit, the stronger the current will be. In Lesson 3, you learned about superconductors, which have no resistance at very low temperatures. Extremely strong electric current can pass through superconductors.

Think about the strength of the electromagnet you made using wire as a conductor. How many paper clips did the electromagnet lift with ten loops of wire around the nail? With 20 loops? Did you also notice that the coils became warm due to electrical energy being converted to heat? Imagine how much stronger an electromagnet receiving current from a superconductor would be if the superconductor lost no electrical energy as heat!

Superconductor technology allows us to create stronger magnets with stronger magnetic fields than ever before. Superconducting magnets are used to run machines called MRIs (Magnetic Resonance Imaging machines), which are used in many hospitals. MRIs allow doctors to use magnets to take pictures of patients' insides without their even feeling it. That's much easier on the patient than surgery!

Sum It Up

You observed an electric current producing a magnetic field when you constructed an electromagnet. You also saw how a magnetic field could cause an electric current when you placed a magnet inside a coil of wire. These observations have given you a clearer picture of the relationship between magnetism and electricity. Many systems that use electrical energy use the magnetic field surrounding a current. Such systems include huge electromagnets, doorbells, cassette tape players, and Magnetic Resonance Imaging machines. In the next lesson, you'll learn how electric motors use the magnetic field surrounding a current. You'll also see how magnetism is used to generate most of the electricity used in the world.

Critical Thinking

1. Imagine you're looking at a road map of the state where you live. On the map is a drawing of a compass face showing the actual relationship of your state to a line running exactly north and south. How could you use the drawing of the compass face and a real magnetic compass to help you find your way on a trip?

2. The end of a compass needle that points north is called the north-seeking pole of the compass. If the compass needle were removed from the compass, would we say that the north-seeking end was the north or the south pole of the magnet? Explain.

3. Why should computer students be warned to keep their computer disks away from magnets?

4. How can you use a compass to locate iron nails in a wall, even years after they've been covered by paint and wallpaper?

5. Imagine that your teacher has given you two bar magnets and has told you that one is still strong but the other has lost its magnetic properties. Without using anything but the two bar magnets, how can you tell which is which? (Hint: Study the diagrams of the lines of force that surround a bar magnet in your **Activity Log**.)

Where Does Electric Power Come From?

*We use electric power to find our way
nearly every hour of every day.
Does this power come from an outlet near the table
or from a large underground cable?
The outlet and cable merely deliver
power from a plant near the river.*

Think about the electrical explorations you've made. The source we use to generate electricity depends on how much electricity we need. A battery was ideal to produce the small amount of current your first explorations of electricity required. By contrast, the power plant supplying electricity for your home generates and transmits huge amounts of electrical energy over long distances. A battery couldn't begin to produce the amount of current a power plant sends out.

Minds On! What different sources of energy produce electric current in power plants? What are the advantages and disadvantages of each source of power? Write your ideas in your **Activity Log** on page 38. ●

You may already know why we call coal, oil, and natural gas "fossil fuels." It's because they're composed of the remains of plants and animals that lived millions of years ago. Coal, oil, and natural gas are also known as nonrenewable resources because we aren't able to make new coal, oil, or natural gas. Once they're used up, they're gone.

A power plant may use chemical energy stored in coal to generate electricity.

72

This substation in Norfolk, Virginia, takes in high-voltage power and sends low-voltage power out to homes and businesses.

EXPLORE Activity!

Putting Electricity To Work

You know that electricity powers golf carts, sewing machines, and many other electrical devices. But do you know how the power in an electric motor is produced? You can construct an electric motor.

What You Need

200 cm of 18-gauge enameled wire
2 D cells with holders
sandpaper
2 giant paper clips
2 25-cm lengths of insulated wires
your switch from Lesson 5
bar magnet
wire strippers
Activity Log pages 39–40

What To Do

1. Make a coil by wrapping the enameled wire 15 times around a D cell.

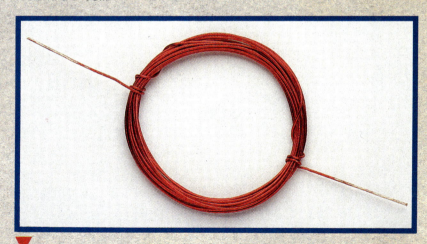

2. Remove the coil from the cell. Loop each free end twice around the center of each side. Leave the ends sticking out as shown. Sandpaper about 1 cm of the enameling from the free ends. Save the coil for step 6.

3. Straighten one side of each of 2 giant paper clips. Leave the other side looped.

4 Stick the straightened ends of the paper clips into the positive end of one cell holder and the negative end of the other cell holder as shown.

5 Fasten one end of 2 25-cm insulated wires onto the opposite side of the cell holders. Fasten the other ends to each end of an open switch.

6 Place the coil in the paper clips as shown. The coil should turn easily. Bring the bar magnet near the coil. Write your observations in your *Activity Log.*

7 Complete the circuit by closing the switch.

8 Pick up the bar magnet and hold one end near the coil. Use your finger to gently spin the coil to start the motor. Move the magnet around until you find the position where the coil spins the fastest. Hold the magnet in this position. Write your observations in your *Activity Log.*

What Happened?

1. Why did you remove the enameling from the ends of the coil wires?
2. How did you make the circuit complete?
3. Make a diagram of the circuit you completed.

What Now?

1. Why do you think the motor turns? (Think about what you learned about electromagnets and magnetic fields in Lesson 6.)
2. Design and carry out an experiment that would change the speed of the spinning coil. Use the steps of the scientific method—state a problem, write a hypothesis, design an experiment that will test your hypothesis, record and analyze the experimental data, and, finally, draw a conclusion. Record your experiment in your *Activity Log.*

EXPLORE

Motors, Generators, and Meters

In the Explore Activity, you constructed an electric motor and observed it in action. Motors change electrical energy into mechanical energy. **Mechanical energy** is the energy of moving parts. Each part of an electric motor has mechanical energy when it's moving. Think about the coil you made for your electric motor. The coil is also an electromagnet when there's a current. What do you suppose would happen if you connected the coil with an iron core directly to a battery and then brought the coil near a pile of iron filings? The coil would attract the iron filings. What if you brought a bar magnet close to the coil while it was connected directly to the battery? The coil would attract and repel the bar magnet causing the motor to turn. Try to explain why.

Minds On! In your *Activity Log* on page 41, list five devices or appliances that use electric motors to do work. Hint: The motors are often hidden inside or behind other parts.

Motors do all kinds of useful work outside and inside the home. Motors turn the blades on fans. They turn the wheels on electric locomotives. They run electric pumps that bring water from outdoor wells into people's homes. Motors differ widely in shape and size, but all motors have coils to produce magnetic fields.

Think about the wheels on an automobile. They turn in a circular motion. Scientists have now produced reliable cars with wheels that are turned by electric motors instead of by burning gasoline.

Think about how electricity and magnetism are related. The same principles we use to make motors also allow us to make generators that produce electricity. A generator is a motor in reverse. You know motors change electrical energy into mechanical energy. **Electrical generators** change mechanical energy into electrical energy. How?

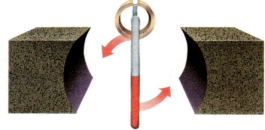

The wire coil begins to turn because on both sides the magnetic fields from the magnet and the wire coil repel each other.

At the gap between negative and positive, the current in the coil reverses direction.

The wire coil continues to turn because the forces on the coil are in the same direction.

Do you remember how Michael Faraday proved that magnetism could produce electricity? Faraday thrust a magnet into the center of a coil of wire. The magnetic field of the magnet caused electrons to move in the wire, and an electric current was produced. Generators use the principles Faraday discovered to change mechanical energy into electrical energy. The generator on this page uses coils of wire and magnets to make electrons move. What happens when electrons move through the wire coils around the circuit?

Like an electric motor, a generator stays on only so long as its coils are spinning through a magnetic field. Notice the generator shaft, or **armature,** which is a coil of wires attached to a handle on one end. As long as someone or something turns the handle on the armature, the coils spin through the magnetic field. Electrons keep moving through the circuit.

Any generator must have a source of mechanical energy to turn the armature and maintain the flow of electrons. In a hand-turned generator, that source could be you! Some small portable generators, such as those on campers, use gasoline engines to turn the armature.

The generators that electric power companies use to change mechanical energy to electricity operate on a much larger scale. Look at the windmills, or turbines, in the generator pictured. The **turbines** are made of many blades and work like the crank that turns the armature in a hand-turned generator. You can infer the generators using these turbines need much more mechanical power than a person's arm can provide! Steam spins the turbines in most power plants. Where does steam come from? In most power plants, coal, oil, or natural gas is burned to boil water for steam. Later in this lesson, you'll see generators that use the power of falling water, windmills, or nuclear reactions to produce electricity.

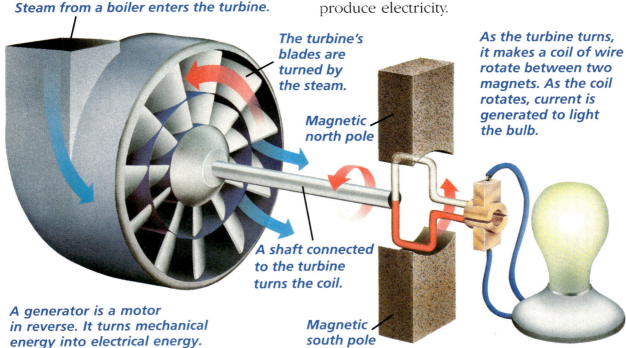

Steam from a boiler enters the turbine.

The turbine's blades are turned by the steam.

Magnetic north pole

As the turbine turns, it makes a coil of wire rotate between two magnets. As the coil rotates, current is generated to light the bulb.

A shaft connected to the turbine turns the coil.

A generator is a motor in reverse. It turns mechanical energy into electrical energy.

Magnetic south pole

77

DC and AC

So far, all of your explorations with electricity have focused on electric current flowing in only one direction. Think about the source of electric current in the motor you made: two flashlight cells. You know that in a cell electrons flow in one direction, from the negative terminal to the positive terminal. The kind of current flowing in only one direction is called **direct current,** or **DC.** When only a small amount of electric current is required, as in the motor that you made, DC works fine.

Power plants generate and transmit huge amounts of energy over long distances. They supply not only households but also offices, schools, stores, hospitals, factories, and fire stations with electricity.

The kind of current running from a power plant to your home is called alternating current. The alternating current coming into your house is at a much higher voltage than the direct current coming from a flashlight battery. The higher voltage makes household current dangerous. **Alternating current,** or **AC,** flows rapidly forward and backward, changing direction 60 times per second. Have you ever seen someone drilling down into the pavement on a street or sidewalk with a jackhammer? The drill on the jackhammer goes rapidly (and noisily!) up and down. You can picture electrons in an alternating current as surging back and forth in the wires like the end of a jackhammer.

Perhaps your school has calculators powered either by a battery or by being plugged into an electrical outlet in the wall. If a battery produces DC and the current that flows in the wires of schools and homes is AC, how can a calculator use either one? Calculators, radios, and many other small, battery-operated electrical devices come with special converters. These **AC/DC converters** plug into the

This tape player operates on DC current. Electrons flow in only one direction in DC current.

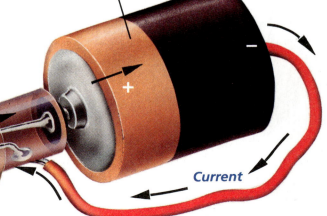

Cells provide DC.

Current

78

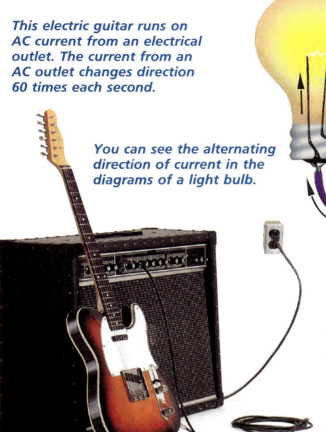

This electric guitar runs on AC current from an electrical outlet. The current from an AC outlet changes direction 60 times each second.

You can see the alternating direction of current in the diagrams of a light bulb.

wall and use diodes to convert the AC from the wall socket into DC that the device can use. In Lesson 3 you observed how a diode will only permit current in one direction.

As you can imagine, the electricity used to operate all the electrical devices described in Lesson 2 isn't free. You pay for it. Actually, you pay for the amount of electrical energy that you use. The more electrical energy you use, the higher your electric bill will be. If you live in a place where the winters are very cold and your home is heated by electricity, the amount you pay can vary tremendously from season to season. Think about how the need for electrical energy varies in the course of only one day. In the morning, when people use electric water heaters, hair dryers, stoves, coffee makers, microwave ovens, and toasters, the demand for electric power is high. In the middle of the night, when most people are asleep, the demand is relatively low.

Ask an adult to show you where the electric meter in your home is located. The electric meter is made up of several small dials and a larger horizontal wheel that turns at different speeds. The meter measures the electrical energy your household uses in units called kilowatt-hours. A watt is the basic unit that we use to measure the amount of electric power it takes to do something such as run a TV set or a computer. A 10-watt bulb uses only a little electric power. A 100-watt bulb is much brighter and uses ten times more power. An electric motor may use several hundred watts—quite a bit more. Kilowatts are units that measure large amounts of electric power. Think about the prefix *kilo-*, which means "one thousand." A kilowatt is 1,000 watts. A **kilowatt-hour** is the amount of energy used when you consume one kilowatt of power in one hour.

79

Electric meters record how many kilowatt-hours of electricity each house is billed for.

The wheel on the electric meter turns quickly or slowly depending on how many kilowatt-hours you use. Watch the wheel at a time during the day when no one is cooking or using any lights. Compare how fast the wheel turns during this low-use time with how fast it turns at the evening mealtime, when much more energy is needed to cook food and light your home. You will notice the wheel turning much faster when more electrical devices are being used.

Every month, the power company that sells electrical energy sends someone to your home or apartment to read the meter and find out the number of kilowatt-hours you used that month. The power company then uses this meter reading to determine your bill.

Paying the Price for Olympic Gold

The Summer Olympic Games take place every four years. For two weeks, people around the world watch the world's best athletes competing for medals. Suppose you watch the Summer Olympic Games on TV for several hours each day. During the two weeks that the games are on, you watch them for a total of 50 hours. Your TV uses 200 watts of electric power. The electric company charges 10 cents for each kilowatt-hour of electric energy. How much does it cost to watch 50 hours of TV on your television?

To solve this problem, begin by changing watts to kilowatts.

200 watts/1,000 watts per kilowatt = 0.20 kW

Then you multiply kilowatts by the number of hours.

0.20 kW × 50 h = 10 kWh

Finally, you multiply kilowatt-hours by the cost per kilowatt-hour.

10 kWh × 10 cents per kWh = 100 cents or $1.00

The electric company will charge you $1.00 for watching the Summer Olympics on TV.

Now, try to figure how many hours your own TV is used during a month. How much does the electricity cost to operate your TV in a month?

Powerful Problems

Remember the circuits you made in Lesson 2? How many volts did the cell you used produce? The power lines that bring electricity from the power plant to your neighborhood contain a whopping 120,000 to 500,000 volts! By the time the power goes into your home, it has been changed, or transformed, to a safer—but still very dangerous— 220 and 120 volts. Read the Literature Link to better appreciate the need to transform electric power before using it in a house.

Look outside your apartment or home this evening. Is there a pole? If so, you may be able to see the actual wires that carry electric current to your home. Safety experts warn everyone to stay away from power lines because of the high voltages and currents carried on power lines. No one should ever touch a power line. Even flying a kite near power lines can be dangerous. The kite string could conduct electricity from the power lines to the ground through you. Remember Benjamin Franklin's experiment? You can't count on having Franklin's good luck!

Literature Link

The Secret Life of Dilly McBean

" 'I want you to be aware of the electrical as well as the magnetic effects. Not just on yourself, but on your surroundings.'

Electrical effects, now there was something to think about. Dilly's forehead puckered in concentration. 'I guess,' he said slowly, 'if the electricity fed into something like a TV, it could knock it out.'

'A gigantic surge could play havoc with an area's power source. Imagine, lights would go off.'

Dilly picked up on the idea. 'So would refrigerators.' "

In Dorothy Haas's *The Secret Life of Dilly McBean,* a teenager named Dilly can attract things to his hands by thinking magnetically.

Imagine you are a superhero named Magnetic Kid. What superpowers would you have? Brainstorm with some classmates to come up with a list. Then write a story or a script in which Magnetic Kid performs wonders using these superpowers. If you like, illustrate your script to create a comic book.

Very high voltages are used to send electricity over long distances.

81

SCIENCE TECHNOLOGY AND Society

Focus on Environment

Go With the Flow?

Generating electric power from water, or **hydroelectric power,** has been viewed by many as an excellent idea. Hydroelectric power is inexpensive to produce, and it does not pollute the air. A renewable resource—water—spins the turbines in hydroelectric power plants. In fact, some people in the United States already depend on hydroelectric power. Hydroelectric plants supply 300 billion kilowatt-hours of electricity per year, meeting 9.5 percent of the U.S.A.'s needs for electricity.

The economic cost of hydroelectric power is relatively low, but many people believe the cost to the environment is dangerously high. Rivers must be dammed to produce hydroelectric power. Imagine a river with a large salmon population. Salmon migrate upstream and downriver each year on a deadline. If they don't meet the deadline, salmon cannot spawn, or reproduce. Dams used to produce hydroelectric power slow the salmon's journey. Even more dangerous for the salmon are hydroelectric turbines that are located in the water. These turbines consist of large rotating metal blades. They can chop up salmon or injure them severely unless a protective screen is used to keep the salmon from the blades.

Hydropower produces other harmful environmental side effects. Dams eliminate the natural flooding cycle of a river on which many animals and plants depend. Hydroelectric turbines flush vast amounts

Hydroelectric power plants use water to spin turbines.

82

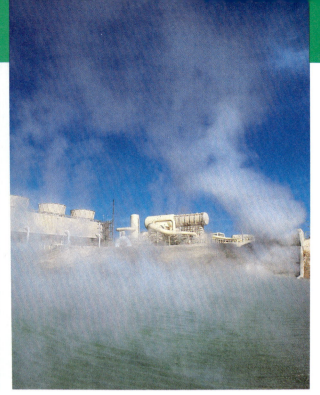

The production of geothermal energy can only occur where hot rocks are close to the surface.

of water into riverbeds whenever the demand for electric power is high.

Scientists and engineers are working hard to find better sources of energy to power the turbines in electric power plants. Why? You know that steam spins the turbines in most power plants. Do you remember how the steam is usually produced? Fossil fuels are burned. It's important for scientists to find alternative ways of generating electricity so the supply of fossil fuels will last longer.

The good news is that scientists have been successful. They have found ways of spinning turbines using the power of the atom, wind, tides, and the heat in Earth itself. The bad news is that there are disadvantages to each of these alternatives.

In a nuclear power plant, atoms are split. The process gives energy that is used to heat water and change it to steam. A large amount of energy can be produced from a relatively small amount of nuclear fuel. However, these plants produce harmful waste products—some that give off dangerous cancer-causing radiation for hundreds of years. So far scientists, engineers, and politicians have not agreed how to dispose of nuclear wastes safely.

If you visit Altamont Pass, California, you can see long rows of giant windmills. These windmills use free and clean wind energy to run electric generators. In France and the Soviet Union, power plants have harnessed the ocean tides to operate generators. Some power plants in Italy and California use heat within Earth, or **geothermal energy,** to make steam for generating electricity.

Wind power, tidal power, and geothermal energy are promising, but not trouble-free, ways to increase our supply of electricity. The amount of power wind can deliver is limited by local weather conditions. Tidal power, like hydropower, uses dams to make new pools and lakes of water. These pools and lakes can be harmful to fish populations and birds that live near the ocean shore. Geothermal power plants have operated for many years without harming the environment. However, geothermal energy can be tapped only in certain "hot spots" where underground steam is found.

Think about how much energy the sun continually gives off. Solar energy in the form of heat and light comes to Earth from the sun. To see how solar energy can be useful, do the Try This Activity.

Each solar cell produces an electric current.

TRY THIS Activity!

Tea From Sunlight
Can sunlight heat water for tea? Let's see!

What You Need
2 identical plastic jars
cold tap water
herbal tea bags
Activity Log page 42

Fill both jars with cold tap water. Record how warm the water feels in your **Activity Log**. Put 3 tea bags in each jar. Set 1 jar in bright sunlight, and set the other jar in the shade. Every 10 minutes, note the color and warmth of the water. After an hour, taste the contents of each jar. Which method made better tea? Which method used solar energy?

Scientists have developed **solar cells,** which are thin strips of a material that produce an electric current when struck by sunlight. You may have seen a watch, radio, or calculator powered by a solar cell. Electrical generating plants have also been built that use solar energy to produce steam for driving turbines. Solar power plants are expensive to build. Perhaps someone will discover a way to use the sun's energy for generating electricity that is less expensive. The search for a way to inexpensively use the sun to generate electricity teaches us a lot about how science works. Many scientists are working in teams trying to solve this problem. Maybe someday you'll be a part of a team that successfully uses the sun's energy as an inexpensive way to generate electricity.

You've seen that solar energy can be useful in tea-making. But bigger projects can also be accomplished with the help of the sun.

✷ Sum It Up ✷

You've constructed an electric motor using current electricity and a bar magnet. Motors change electrical energy into mechanical energy. You've also learned about generators. Generators convert mechanical energy into electrical energy. Electrical energy travels as two types of current: AC and DC. AC (alternating current), which flows rapidly backward and forward and changes direction 60 times per second, is used to supply power from power plants to homes. DC (direct current), which flows only in one direction, is often used for smaller electric power needs that use a battery as the source of energy.

The world is using more and more energy in the form of electricity. The costs and benefits of the various ways we have of generating electricity are being studied. Information from these studies will help us keep electrical systems operating while preserving Earth's natural resources.

Critical Thinking

1. What effect would it have on a motor if you used additional batteries to drive it? Explain your answer.

2. Most motorized toys use small electric motors powered by one or two batteries. Since the only moving part of a motor is the spinning shaft, how can motors make toys walk, crawl, fold, and lift?

3. Imagine you've just invented a system you call the Forever Motor System. You've connected a motor in series with a generator so that when the motor turns, the crank of the generator also turns. The generator then makes electricity to run the motor. Your hypothesis is that once started, the Forever Motor System will run forever on no fuel at all, and you'll become rich and famous. Is your hypothesis correct? Explain your answer.

4. You and a friend are having a friendly argument. He knows your home is heated by burning oil. His home is heated by electricity. He says his home's heating system doesn't pollute the air, while yours does. Who is right? Explain.

5. Car batteries last for years. Since so many parts of a car run on electricity, how can the battery last so long? Why does a car battery "die" in just an hour or so if you leave the headlights on with the motor turned off?

Theme — ENERGY

Electricity at Home

You know electric current begins its journey to houses and apartment buildings at a power station. The illustration on these pages shows the route electric current takes into and around one home.

Notice the pole and the metal box labeled *transformer*. The transformer lowers the high voltage coming from the power station to the much lower voltage that house circuits carry. Locate the wires bringing electric current into the house.

Look inside the house shown. Notice the places where electrical outlets are located.

Minds On! Think about the electrical outlets in your living room. In your **Activity Log** on page 43, draw a diagram of your living room and its electrical outlets. •

Today most houses and apartments with electricity have 100- or 200-amp electrical service. This means the total current supplied to electrical appliances and devices used in the entire house can equal no more than 100 or 200 amps. An iron uses eight amps. A coffee pot uses about seven amps. If a kitchen circuit carried 20 amps, could you use the iron and coffee pot at the same time on this 20-amp circuit?

When your grandparents were children, most house circuits could supply a total of only 40 amps. Some older houses in rural areas still have just 40 amps of total capacity. Think about what effect this lower current has on the number and kind of electrical devices that can be used at one time by people who live in such homes. Cooking in a microwave oven, which uses about 10 amps, would probably blow the fuses in the kitchen circuit if the lights were also turned on. In fact, it's a good idea to know which circuits control which outlets. Do the Try This Activity to map your home's circuits in case of an electrical emergency.

TRY THIS Activity!

Your Home's Circuits

What You Need
paper and pencil
adult family member
your home's fuse box or breaker panel
small electrical appliance, such as a lamp
Activity Log page 44

In your **Activity Log**, draw a floor plan of your home. Show the location of each electrical outlet. With the adult family member, find the fuse box or circuit breaker panel. If each fuse or circuit breaker isn't already numbered, number it. Have the adult family member turn off 1 fuse or circuit breaker. Go through your home and test each outlet with the small appliance to find those outlets that no longer work. On your floor plan, write the number of the fuse or circuit breaker near the outlet it controls. Repeat this process until all the fuses or circuit breakers have been tested. After class discussion, tape your floor plan to the inside of the fuse box or breaker panel for future reference.

Minds On! Talk to one of your grandparents or to someone else who remembers life in the 1940s. Ask if they remember how many total amps of current were supplied to their house. Also, ask them which electrical devices and appliances they remember using during the 1940s. What problems did they have if several devices were used at the same time? Write what they tell you in your *Activity Log* on page 45. Compare your information with the information gathered by your classmates.

The electrical devices used in homes during the 1940s may seem very different from today's electrical devices. Have you ever considered how different it would be with no electrical devices in a home? Read the following Social Studies Link to learn more about people who choose not to use electricity in their homes.

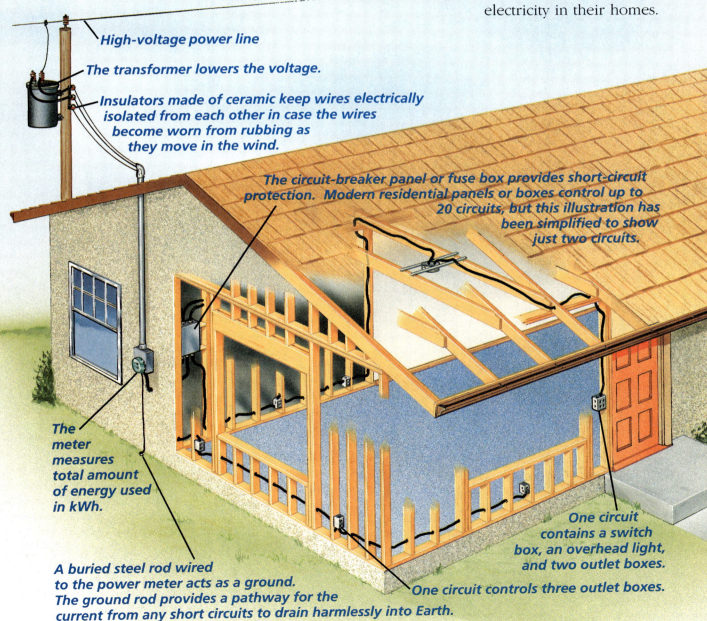

Social Studies Link

Choosing Not To Use Electricity

You know that the United States is a multicultural society. Some Americans are native to this land, while other Americans have their family roots in African cultures, Asian cultures, European cultures, or they may originate from some other part of the world. Americans also have different religious heritages and beliefs. Some Americans practice Buddhism, Judaism, Christianity, Hinduism, Native American religions, Islam, or other beliefs. Some Americans practice no religion at all. If you travel across our country, you can observe many different ways of life.

In this unit, we've assumed that electricity is a good thing when it is available because it makes our lives safer, healthier, easier, and more enjoyable. This assumption is widely—but not unanimously—shared by people in the United States.

Suppose you traveled to an Amish community in Lancaster County, Pennsylvania. You'd see people wearing handmade clothes fastened with hooks and eyes instead of buttons. The Amish religion teaches that the older and simpler ways of life bring people closer to each other.

The Amish want nothing to do with most electrical appliances and devices. They light their homes with gas lanterns rather than electric lights. Gas is also used instead of electricity to heat water and run refrigerators and stoves in Amish homes. The Amish do not use electric dryers to dry their hair or use TVs, VCRs, or radios to entertain their children.

Electricity is not entirely absent from Amish life. They put flashing, red electric lights on the backs of their horse-drawn buggies to warn approaching traffic that a slow vehicle is moving down the road. Many Amish are farmers. Some use electric fences for keeping cattle in pastures, electric power saws for building, and electrically-powered bulk storage tanks to hold the milk that they sell to dairies.

The Amish wear electronic hearing aids if they need them. Elderly people in the community are permitted to use battery-powered lamps to read. But in homes and family life, the Amish use electricity only when they must. The Amish fear that all the conveniences provided by electricity will not allow them to maintain a simple, traditional, family-centered, and community-centered way of life.

Can you think of any other reasons people might choose to live without electricity? What are electricity's advantages and disadvantages as you see them? What positive and negative changes have occurred in countries around the world because of electricity? Write your thoughts in a short essay.

What modern electrical devices have the Amish people in these photographs chosen not to use?

GLOSSARY

Use the pronunciation key below to help you decode, or read, the pronunciations.

Pronunciation Key

a	at, bad		d	dear, soda, bad
ā	ape, pain, day, break		f	five, defend, leaf, off, cough, elephant
ä	father, car, heart		g	game, ago, fog, egg
âr	care, pair, bear, their, where		h	hat, ahead
e	end, pet, said, heaven, friend		hw	white, whether, which
ē	equal, me, feet, team, piece, key		j	joke, enjoy, gem, page, edge
i	it, big, English, hymn		k	kite, bakery, seek, tack, cat
ī	ice, fine, lie, my		l	lid, sailor, feel, ball, allow
îr	ear, deer, here, pierce		m	man, family, dream
o	odd, hot, watch		n	not, final, pan, knife
ō	old, oat, toe, low		ng	long, singer, pink
ô	coffee, all, taught, law, fought		p	pail, repair, soap, happy
ôr	order, fork, horse, story, pour		r	ride, parent, wear, more, marry
oi	oil, toy		s	sit, aside, pets, cent, pass
ou	out, now		sh	shoe, washer, fish mission, nation
u	up, mud, love, double		t	tag, pretend, fat, button, dressed
ū	use, mule, cue, feud, few		th	thin, panther, both
ü	rule, true, food		<u>th</u>	this, mother, smooth
u̇	put, wood, should		v	very, favor, wave
ûr	burn, hurry, term, bird, word, courage		w	wet, weather, reward
ə	about, taken, pencil, lemon, circus		y	yes, onion
b	bat, above, job		z	zoo, lazy, jazz, rose, dogs, houses
ch	chin, such, match		zh	vision, treasure, seizure

alternating current (AC) (ôl′ tər nāt′ ing): a continuous back-and-forth movement of electrons in a circuit; current that changes direction

ampere (am′ pîr′): the rate of electron flow in a circuit; the unit of current

armature (är′ mə chər′): coil of wire around a metal core, in which electric current interacts with a magnetic field to produce torque in a motor

attracted: having been pulled or drawn

circuit (sür′ kit): a closed-loop path of conduction through which an electric current flows

circuit breaker: device that stops the flow of current before wires in a circuit can become too hot; a strip of metal that bends when heated and allows a spring to open a switch

closed circuit: a complete path for electric current

conduct (kən dukt′): to transmit electricity

conductor (kən duk′ tər): material through which electrons can move

contact: the junction of two electrical conductors through which a current passes

continuity tester (kon′ tə nü′ ə tē): a device with an open space in the circuit to test conductivity

converter, AC/DC: a device with a diode that changes AC to DC

90

current electricity: the flow of electrons through a material

declination (dek′ lə nā′ shən): the angle formed by the magnetic needle of a compass and a line between Earth's magnetic poles; a measurement that tells how much to adjust a compass to point to true north

diode (dī′ ōd′): a conductor through which electricity can flow in only one direction

direct current (DC): flow of electrons in one direction of current through a conductor

discharge: a loss of negative or positive electric charge

domain (do mān′): the region inside a material in which the magnetic fields of all spinning, unpaired electrons point in the same direction

electrical generator (i lek′ tri kəl jen′ ə rā′ tər): a source of current that uses a coil of wire turning in a magnetic field

electrically neutral: having the same number of positive and negative charges

electric charge: having too many or too few electrons

electromagnet (i lek′ trō mag′ nit): a soft iron core surrounded by a wire coil through which an electric current is passed, thus magnetizing the core

electron (i lek′ tron′): a negatively-charged particle that moves around the nucleus of an atom

electroplater (i lek′ trə plā tûr): a person who employs electrodeposition to put a coating of metal on the surface of a conductor

electroplating: the use of an electric current to tive the surface of a conductor a coating of metal

fuse: safety device that stops the flow of current before wires become too hot; contains a small piece of fusible metal that melts and breaks the circuit when the current exceeds a certain amperage

geothermal energy (jē′ ō thûr′ məl): heat from within Earth

ground: the connection of an object to Earth by an electrical conductor to allow electrons to move into Earth

Ground Fault Circuit Interrupter (GFCI): a very sensitive kind of circuit breaker than prevents electrical shock

grounded: having a pathway for static discharges to flow to Earth

hydroelectric power (hī′ drō i lek′ trik pou′ ər): electric power generated by moving water

insulator (in′ sə lā′ tər): a substance through which electricity cannot flow readily

kilowatt-hour (kWh) (kil′ ə wot′): a unit used to measure electrical energy; equal to 1000 watt-hours

lightning rod: a metallic rod set up on a building and connected with Earth whose purpose is to ground the large, destructive static discharges of lightning

lodestone (lōd′ stōn′): a naturally-occurring mineral, magnetite (iron oxide), possessing magnetic properties

magnetic field (mag net′ ik fēld): area of magnetic lines of force

mechanical energy (mi kan′ i kəl): the kinetic energy and potential energy of lifting, bending, and stretching

negatively charged: having an excess of electrons

neutron (nü′ tron′): particle with no charge having 1800 times the mass of an electron, located in the nucleus of an atom

ohm (ōm): unit for measuring electric resistance

Ohm's Law: a scientific law stating that the strength of a current is equal to the voltage divided by the resistance of the circuit

open circuit: an incomplete path that will not permit an electric current to flow

parallel circuit: a circuit in which two or more devices are connected across two common points in the circuit to provide separate conducting paths for the current

positively charged: having a shortage of electrons

potential difference: the difference in potential energy between charges in two different locations; voltage

printed circuit: a conductor printed on the surface of a piece of plastic

proton (prō′ ton′): positively-charged particle in the nucleus of an atom

repel (ri pel′): to force away or apart

resistance (ri zis′ təns): any opposition that slows down or prevents movement of electrons through a conductor; opposition to the flow of electricity

semiconductor (sem′ ē kən duk′ tər): a material with a resistance between that of a conductor and an insulator; that which conducts electric current weakly

separation of charges (sep′ ə rā′ shən): the moving part of positive and negative charges in a neutral object

series circuit: an electric circuit in which the parts are connected so that the current flows through each part of the circuit one after another

short circuit: a low-resistance connection between two points in an electric circuit, resulting in a side circuit that deflects most of the current from desired paths; an excessive current flow that often causes damage

solar cell: photovoltaic cell used as a power source converting sunlight into electrical energy

static charge: a charge that stays in one place

static discharge: loss of static electricity

static electricity: electricity produced by charged bodies; charge built up in one place

superconductor (sü′ pər kən duk′ tər): a conductor that has no electrical resistance at temperatures near absolute zero

turbine: rotary engine, usually large, in which steam or water powers the blades

voltage (vōl′ tij): potential difference; the difference of potential between two points

volt (vōlt): the SI unit of electric potential

INDEX

AC/DC converters, 78–79
Alternate energy sources, 82–84
Alternating current (AC), 78–79, *illus.,* 79
Amish communities, 88–89
Amperes, 29
Animals, navigation, 68
Armature, 77
Attracting forces, 14; *act.,* 12–13, 15
Automobiles, electrical systems, 48–49

Batteries, 46–48, *act.,* 26, 44–45, 46
Ben and Me (Lawson), 9
Billings, Charlene, 9
Blinkers and Buzzers (Zubrowski), 9
Blood flow, 27, 37; *illus.,* 27, 37
Bones, recharging, 30
Book reviews, 8–9

Cars, electrical systems, 48–49
Charges, 10, 12–19; *act.,* 12–13, 15
Chinese discoveries, 61, 66
Circuit breakers, 56–58; *act.,* 56; *illus.,* 56
Circuits, 20, 22–31; *act.,* 22–23, 52–53, 86; closed, 24; *act.,* 25; control of, 50, 52–59; in the home, 86–87; *illus.,* 87; models, 26; *act.,* 22–23; open, 24–25; parallel, 46–49, 55; *act.,* 44–45, 46; *illus.,* 55; printed, 39; series, 46–49, 55–56, *act.,* 44–45, 46; *illus.,* 46, 47, 55; shorts in, 55–56; size of, 39
Circulatory system, 27, 37; *illus.,* 27, 37
Closed circuits, 24–25; *illus.,* 24
Compasses, 66, 68; *act.,* 67; *illus.,* 61; history of, 61
Conductors, 32, 34–41; *act.,* 34–35, 52–53; *illus.,* 36
Contact, static charges, 14
Continuity testers, 36
Crime, electronics and, 70
Current electricity, 20, 22–31; *act.,* 22–23; calculating, 29; direction, 78–79; *illus.,* 78, 79

Declination, 67
Diodes, 37, 79; *act.,* 34–35
Direct current (DC), 78–79; *illus.,* 78
Discharge rates, *act.,* 46
Domain, magnetic, 65

Earth, magnetic field, 66–67, *illus.,* 67
Electrical charges, 10, 12–19

Electrical systems, automobiles, 48–49
Electric eels, 16; *illus.,* 16
Electric generators, 68, 76–77; *illus.,* 77
Electricity, costs, 79–80; *act.,* 80; current, 20, 22–31, 78–79; disadvantages, 88–89; in the home, 47, 50, 58, 78, 79, 80, 86–87; *act.,* 86, 87; interruption, 50, 52–59; and magnetism, 60–70; *act.,* 62–63, 68; medical uses, 30; safety measures, 16, 17, 36–37, 54–56, 81; static, 10–19; transmission, 12; uses for, 6, 20, 30, 88–89
Electric meters, 79–80; *illus.,* 80
Electric motors, 76; *act.,* 74–75; *illus.,* 76
Electromagnets, 64, 71; *act.,* 62–63; *illus.,* 64
Electronic service technicians, 69
Electronic surveillance, 70
Electrons, 6–7; interruption, 50, 52–59; *act.,* 52–53; pathways, 42, 44–49; *act.,* 44–45
Electroplaters, 40
Electroplating, 40; *act.,* 39
Energy sources, 82–84
Environment, electricity production effects on, 82–83

93

INDEX continued

Fainting, 57; *act.,* 57
Faraday, Michael, 68, 77
Fire prevention, 37, 54–56
Fossil fuels, 72, 83
Franklin, Benjamin, 18–19
Fuses, 56, 58

Generators, 68, 76–77; *illus.,* 77
Geothermal energy, 83
Gravity, 7
Grounding, electrical, 16, 17
Gutnik, Martin J., 9

Haas, Dorothy, 8, 81
Heat, and resistance, 29, 38
Hydroelectric power, 82–83

Insulators, 36–37; *illus.,* 36

Kilowatt-hours, 79–80

Lawson, Robert, 9
Lightning, 16, 17, 18–19; *illus.,* 16
Lightning rods, 17, 18

Magnetic fields, 64–65, 66; *act.,* 65; *illus.,* 66; of Earth, 66–67; *illus.,* 67
Magnetism, and electricity, 60–71 *act.,* 62–63, 68; navigation aid, 67, 68; uses for, 60–61, 64, 67, 68, 69, 71
Magnetite, 68

Math, Irwin, 9, 41
Mechanical energy, 76–77

Navigation, 67, 68; by animals, 68; history of, 61
Neutrons, 6–7
Nonrenewable resources, 72
Nuclear power plants, 83

Oersted, Hans Christian, 68
Ohm, Georg S., 28
Ohms, 28, 29
Ohm's Law, 28, 29–30, 47, 55
Open circuits, 24–25; *illus.,* 24

Parallel circuits, 46–49, 55; *act.,* 44–45, 46; *illus.,* 46, 55
Potential difference, 25; *act.,* 26
Power lines, 81, *illus.,* 81
Power plants, 72, 77, 82–84
Printed circuits, 39; *illus.,* 39
Protons, 6–7

Repelling forces, 14; *act.,* 12–13, 15
Resistance, 28; and heat, 29, 38

Safety, with electricity, 16, 17, 36–37, 54–56, 81
Salmon, hydropower and, 82

Secret Life of Dilly McBean, The (Haas), 8, 81
Semiconductors, 37
Series circuits, 46–49, 55–56; *act.,* 44–45, 46; *illus.,* 46, 47, 55
Short circuits, 55–56
Simple Electrical Devices (Gutnik) 9
Solar cells, 84; *illus.,* 84
Solar energy, 84; *act.,* 84
Static discharges, 16, 17, 18, 19; *act.,* 18
Static electricity, 10, 12–19; *act.,* 12–13, 15, 18; *illus.,* 7, 10, 11, 14
Superconductivity (Billings), 9
Superconductors, 38, 41, 71
Surveillance, electronic, 70
Switches, 54–56; *act.,* 52–53; *illus.,* 54

Tidal power, 83
Transformers, 86
Turbines, 77, 82; *illus.,* 77

Voltage, 25, 29; *act.,* 26

Watts, 79–80
Windmills, 83
Wires, 29, 32, 36–37
Wires and Watts (Math), 9, 41

Zubrowski, Bernie, 9

94

CREDITS

Photo Credits:
cover, ©Don Landwehrle/The Image Bank; **1,** ©George C. Anderson/1991; **3,** (t) ©Studiohio/1991; (b) ©Comstock; **5,** ©Studiohio/1991; **7,** ©Phil Jude/Science Photo Library/Photo Researchers, Inc.; **8-9,** ©Studiohio/1991; **10,** ©Brent Turner/BLT Productions/1991; **11-14,** ©Studiohio/1991; **15,** (t) ©Brent Turner/BLT Productions/1991; (b) ©Studiohio/1991; **17,** ©Mary Ann Evans/Evans Images; **20-21,** ©George C. Anderson/1991; **22,** Ken Karp for MMSD; **24,** ©KS Studios/1991; **25,** ©George C. Anderson/1991; **26,** ©Werner H. Muller, Peter Arnold, Inc.; **28,** ©Doug Martin/1991; **29,** ©George C. Anderson/1991; **30 - 32,** ©Brent Turner/BLT Productions/1991; **33,** ©Ken Biggs/Tony Stone Worldwide; **34-36,** ©Brent Turner/BLT Productions/1991; **37,** (l) Brent Turner/BLT Productions/1991; (r) K. Pruitt/Custom Medical Stock Photo; **38,** ©W. Marin/Phototake; **39,** (t) ©Peter Steiner/The Stock Market; (b) ©Studiohio/1991; **40,** ©Brent Turner/BLT Productions/1991; **43-46,** ©KS Studios/1991; **47,** ©Doug Martin/1991; **48,** ©General Motors; **50-51,** ©George C. Anderson/1991; **53,** ©KS Studios/1991; **56,** (t) Norman Owen Tomalin/Bruce Coleman; (b) ©George C. Anderson/1991; **57,** ©KS Studios/1991; **58,** ©George C. Anderson/1991; **60,** ©Brent Turner/BLT Productions/1991; **61,** ©George C. Anderson/1991; **62-63,** Ken Karp for MMSD; **65,** ©Brent Turner/BLT Productions/1991; **68,** ©Don King/The Image Bank; **69-72,** ©Brent Turner/BLT Productions/1991; **73,** ©Comstock; **74-75,** Ken Karp for MMSD; **78,** ©Brent Turner/BLT Productions/1991; **79,** ©Studiohio/1991; **80,** ©Doug Martin/1991; **81,** ©David Barnes/The Stock Market; **82,** ©Comstock; **83,** William James Warren/Westlight; **84,** ©Marcello Bertinetti/Photo Researchers, Inc.; **88-89,** ©Martin Rogers/Stock Boston/1986; **88,** ©Blair Seitz/Seitz & Seitz; **89,** ©Blair Seitz/Seitz & Seitz.

Illustration Credits:
14, 16 (t), Kathy Kelleher; **16 (b), 42, 67,** Bill Boyer; **18,** Clint Hansen; **27,** Stephanie Pershing; **47, 87,** James Shough; **54, 55, 64, 76, 77, 78, 79,** Henry Hill; **66,** Bill Singleton

95